Piers Plowman and Christian Allegory

To Elizabeth Salter
and Derek Pearsall

Piers Plowman and Christian Allegory

David Aers

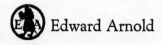 Edward Arnold

First published 1975 by
Edward Arnold (Publishers) Ltd.,
25 Hill Street, London W1X 8LL

ISBN 0 7131 5770 4

Printed in Great Britain by
William Clowes & Sons, Limited
London, Beccles and Colchester

Contents

Preface	vii
Abbreviations	viii
1 Introduction	1
2 Christian Allegory	15
3 Preachers and Poets	33
4 Shells and Kernels: Models of Allegory	52
5 Piers Plowman: Allegorical Modes and Visionary Organization	71
Select Bibliography	132
Index	139

Preface

Some students, who have not had to come to *Piers Plowman* through the scholastic controversies of the last twenty-five years, would probably find it is best to leave the first chapter till last, for this puts the problematic of my own work into the scholastic context.

My greatest thanks in thinking about the subject of this book and in writing it are to Elizabeth Salter and Derek Pearsall, whose boundless intellectual generosity, constant criticism, encouragement and friendship are responsible for its completion.

Abbreviations

AFP	*Archivum Fratrum Praedicatorum*
AHDLMA	*Archives d'histoire doctrinale et literaire du Moyen Age*
Allegorical Imagery	Rosemond Tuve, *Allegorical Imagery: Some Medieval Books and their Posterity.* Princeton, 1966
CHL	*Commentationes Humanarum Litterarum*
CL	*Comparative Literature*
CCSL	*Corpus Christianorum, series latina.* Turnholti
Denis the Carthusian	*Dionysii Carthusiani Enarrationes pia ac eruditae.* 8 vols., Cologne, 1531–5
EC	*Essays in Criticism.*
EETS	*Early English Texts Society*
ES	*Essays and Studies*
Exégèse	H. de Lubac, *Exégèse Mediévale: Les Quatre Sens De L'Ecriture.* 4 vols., Paris, 1959–63.
JEGP	*Journal of English and Germanic Philology*
JR	*Journal of Religion*
JTS	*Journal of Theological Studies*
JWCI	*Journal of the Warburg and Courtauld Institutes*
M Aev	*Medium Aevum*
MLN	*Modern Language Notes*
MLQ	*Modern Language Quarterly*
M Phil	*Modern Philology*
Nicholas of Lyra	Nicholas of Lyra, *Postillae.* 6 vols., Basle, 1506–8
NRT	*Nouvelle Revue Théologique*
PBA	*Proceedings of the British Academy*

PG	*Patrologia, series graeca*, ed.J.-P. Migne. Paris, 1857 ff.
P. Lat.	*Patrologia, series latina*, ed.J.-P. Migne. Paris, 1844 ff.
Pèlerinage	Guillaume de Deguileville, *Pèlerinage de l'Ame*, ed. J. Sturzinger. London, 1895
Pilgrimage	[Lydgate's] Deguileville's *Pilgrimage of the Life of Man*, ed. F. J. Furnivall. EETS, e.s., 77, 83, 92, 1899, 1904
PMLA	*Publications of the Modern Language Association of America*
Preface	D. W. Robertson, Jr., *A Preface to Chaucer. Studies in Medieval Perspectives*. Princeton, 1963
RB	*Revue Biblique*
REA	*Revue des Études Augustiniennes*
R Phil	*Romance Philology*
RR	*Romanic Review*
RSR	*Recherches de Science Religieuse*
RT	*Revue Thomiste*
RTAM	*Recherches de Théologie Ancienne et Médiévale*
SJT	*Scottish Journal of Theology*
SP	*Studies in Philology*
Spec	*Speculum*
ST	*Summa Theologiae*

1 Introduction

There is no learned man but will confess he hath much profited by reading controversies, his senses awaked, his judgements sharpened, and the truth which he holds more firmly established.

Milton, *Of True Religion*

Let the Indefinite be explored . . .
For Art and Science cannot exist but in minutely organized
    Particulars
And not in generalizing Demonstrations . . .

Blake, *Jerusalem* Pl. 55

The aim of this book is to provide a sound basis for reading and interpreting *Piers Plowman*. The approach, in conjunction with the materials explored, also stands as a critical preface to Christian allegory in the Middle Ages. I believe that much controversy about the interpretation of *Piers Plowman* grows out of a failure to subject medieval practices of figural writing and reading to a close critical examination. While there has been abundant assertion and argument about the theory and practice of medieval exegesis (i.e., Biblical commentary) in relation to literature, there has also been a remarkable absence of careful investigation in these areas. One of the intentions of my study is to resolve the long-standing debate about the relations between exegesis, homily and poetry, and in so doing to establish a critical framework within which the particular modes and organization of Langland's allegory will be seen and understood. In my approach the distinction between exegetical theory and exegetical practice is fundamental. We must always be aware of the possibility that verbal practice may not coincide with dogmatic formula, the literary product may not embody the convictions an author would like to believe he is conveying. In fact, the mode of expression is an integral part of the ideas which the author communicates and our interpretation and evaluation must always remain alert to this. Literary criticism is concerned with doctrine and theology, whether among exegetes or poets, only *in relation to* the literary produce, and this obliges us to resist those critics who confuse dogmatic theory with what is actually produced by figurative writers and interpreters. Any meaningful statements about the relationships between exegesis and poetry must present a critical analysis which takes such distinctions into account. With this in mind, I shall submit the practices of exegetical allegory to a critical analysis and I shall do the same with the preachers' allegory before moving onto questions of poetic allegory and a detailed exploration of Langland's own allegorical modes. Continually, close reading must be brought to bear on the relevant works. In my arguments with various scholars I shall return to this standpoint again and again, for failure to observe so basic a requirement has vitiated discussion of medieval figurative modes.

The controversy about medieval allegory and its relations to exegesis has flowed between the poles represented by D. W. Robertson and his opponents. I will begin by considering Robertson's position. He is confident that vernacular literature was read in the same way as Scripture, making both *Piers Plowman* and medieval homilies "derivatives from the exegetical tradition". Robertson has elaborated his views at length but they have not undergone important change since his first essay on the subject when he insisted that "all serious poetry written by Christian authors, even that usually called 'secular', is always allegorical when the message of charity or some corollary of it is not evident on the surface."[1] Robertson claims that medieval writers and interpreters became so conditioned by methods of exegesis that they applied them to all writing and interpretation, including their own:

> During the course of the Middle Ages, literary allegory, although it remained a distinct entity, became closely associated with the allegorical interpretation of the Scriptures. . . . . Meanwhile, the underlying logic of the four senses of Scripture became a habit of mind, and we find preachers like Brinton giving "mystical" or "spiritual" interpretations of materials which have no connection with the Scripture whatsoever.[2]

---

[1] D. W. Robertson and B. F. Huppé, *Piers Plowman and Scriptural Tradition* (Princeton, 1951), 2, 16. See too his other relevant works: "Historical Criticism", in *English Institute Essays* for 1950 (New York, 1951), 3–31; "Some Medieval Literary Terminology", *SP*, 48 (1951), 669–92; "The Doctrine of Charity in Medieval Literary Gardens", *Spec*, 26 (1951), 24–49; A *Preface to Chaucer* (Princeton, 1963), hereafter referred to as *Preface*; and with B. F. Huppé, *Fruyt and Chaf* (Princeton, 1963).

[2] See *Preface*, 289, 335; also forcefully maintained by R. E. Kaske in *Critical Approaches to Medieval Literature*, ed. D. Bethurum (New York, 1960), 27, 30; confirmed by J. B. Allen, *The Friar as Critic* (Nashville, 1971), 4–6, 24–5, 42–59, 73 ff. The implications of this are discussed below; critics who have contradicted Robertson's views here are mistaken: see chapter two and H. de Lubac, *Exégèse Médiévale: Less Quatre Sens de l'Ecriture*, 4 vols. (Paris, 1959–63), II.2.182–233, hereafter cited as *Exégèse*.

Developing his investigation, he says that "'events' in Romanesque art take place in a confined space and time, an area set apart for the representation of symbols which are quite distinct from what we think of as 'real' events." The same applied to "Gothic artists" and, in his opinion, it also seems true of exegesis, in which the Bible is interpreted to show the omnipresence of "the spirit as it was revealed in the acts and teachings of Christ". The instrument of revelation is allegory, and to Robertson the relationship between "the spirit" disclosed by allegory and Old Testament history is analogous with the relationship between Plato's ideal city and the earthly city.[3] Here Robertson makes some striking observations about allegory's treatment of time:

> Thus allegory has the effect of reducing the events of the Old Testament, the New Testament, and one's own actions, together with those of contemporaries, to a kind of continuous present. . . . There is a sense in which the spiritual understanding of Christian allegory produces a similar effect, so that temporal sequence acquires something of the nature of an illusion . . . The same treatment of time frequently appears in medieval literary texts.[4]

The idea that time is something of an illusion is of course a venerable notion.[5] But it is rather unusual to attribute such treatment of time and history to writers in the orthodox Christian tradition. Most students have tended to agree with J. McIntyre that "it is now [1957] a theological commonplace to emphasize the fact that Christianity is an historical religion."[6] In a book devoted to tracing this commonplace, C. A. Patrides began by separating hellenic and Judaeo-Christian notions of time. To the former, time is cyclic and history only consists of "opportunities for didacticism", whereas to the latter time is linear and history is the the area of unique events and "God's 'covenant' with Israel". From this stance Christ's birth "was not the commencement but the climactic point in God's gradual revelation to the people of Israel". Such a view of history, he pointed out, is teleological.[7] These notions have been accepted for a long time and countless scholars have stressed the contrast between

---

[3] See *Preface*, 33–51, 170, 196, 271, 276–7, 290–4; I quote from 161–2 and 292.
[4] *Preface*, 301.
[5] Eliade, "Le temps et l'éternité dans la pensée Indienne", *Eranos Jahrbuch*, 20 (1951), 219–52; Eliade, *The Myth of the Eternal Return* (New York, 1954), 36, 86, and the first two chapters especially. For a neoplatonic view, Plotinus, *The Enneads*, III.6.14 and III.7.
[6] J. McIntyre, *The Christian Doctrine of History* (Edinburgh, 1957), 3.
[7] *The Phoenix and the Ladder* (Berkeley, 1964), 1–7, 8, 14, 16–17, 22, 31 ff.

Christian commitment to history and the anti-historical nature of myth and theology in other religions.[8]

It must be acknowledged that the "theological commonplace" under discussion had its own life in medieval theology. This has been thoroughly documented by H. de Lubac, who describes the importance attached to history and event in the theory of Christian exegesis.[9] His monumental *Exégèse Médiévale* demonstrates how earlier exegetes were quite as insistent as St Thomas Aquinas that any spiritual (allegorical) understanding of the Bible must be built on a sound appreciation of its historical basis. Indeed, Gregory's advice that exegetes should lay a firm historical foundation ("fundamentum historiae") was repeated throughout the Middle Ages.[10] Foundations are not ends in themselves, and the foundation of history is laid to support the walls and roof of allegory and tropology. In this way we see how the theory recorded by de Lubac, expressing the "theological commonplace" of Christianity's historical claims, can, again in theory, accord with the judgement that medieval exegesis was "essentially and universally allegoric".[11]

From the "theological commonplace" being outlined, grows the medieval distinction between Christian allegory ("the allegory of the theologians", "the allegory of things") and the allegory of the poets ("the allegory of words"). Here the theory was that Christian allegory is uniquely an allegory of historical events: man can only dispose words and fictions, whereas God can accommodate events to yield significance.[12] In passing, it is worth noting that one aspect of this theory will be particularly relevant to the culminating chapter on *Piers Plowman*—the idea that allegory centres on Christ, who both unlocked and created the divine meaning of the Old Testament. His acts were the culmination of God's work in time, and in the Incarnation he reveals that "he is the whole content of Scripture, as he contains it all in himself." Christ is the exegete, Christ is the exegized, and the Incarnation becomes the key to the theory of Christian allegory.[13]

---

[8] For example, J. Daniélou: "The Conception of History in the Christian Tradition", *JR*, 30 (1950), 171–9; "The Problem of Symbolism", *Thought*, 25 (1950), 423–40; *From Shadows to Reality* (London, 1960); T. Preiss, "The Christian Philosophy of History", *JR*, 30 (1950), 157–70; E. C. Rust, *The Christian Understanding of History* (London, 1947); K. Lowith, *Meaning in History* (Chicago, 1949).

[9] By de Lubac: *Histoire et Esprit* (Paris, 1950); "'Typologie' et 'Allégorisme'", *RSR*, 34 (1947), 180–226; "À Propos de l'Allégorie Chrétienne", *RSR*, 47 (1959), 5–43.

[10] *Exégèse*, I.1. chapters 3–4; I.2. chapter 7 and 507–21, and II.1.99–197.

[11] *Exégèse*, II.2.41–60; C. Spicq, *Esquisse d'une Histoire de l'Exégèse Latine au Moyen Age* (Paris, 1944), 16 (my trans); on St Thomas's thought on the spiritual sense of the Bible see Mailhiot's article in *RT*, 59 (1959), 613–33.

[12] This reasoning was universal, for some examples see *Exégèse*, II.2.89–93.

[13] *Exégèse*, I.1.318, 322; also I.1.305–63; I.2.373–548; II.2.125–49.

Although I shall make important qualifications to this "theological commonplace" in the coming pages, its centrality in Christian doctrine is unquestionable. It is thus very odd that Robertson does not examine its relationship to his own position rather carefully. His lapse here has encouraged his opponents to challenge his own interpretive methods by applying our "theological commonplace" to medieval allegory.[14] With what justice they have done so, remains to be seen, but Robertson has failed to elucidate the importance of his divergences from more conventional commentaries on Christian approaches to time and history. I stress the importance of his divergences because it seems to me that their content is not entirely eccentric. I hope to demonstrate this in chapter two, but one must recognize a damaging *lacuna* in Robertson's case.

Before surveying the arguments of his opponents, perhaps I should comment on a related inadequacy in Robertson's critical approach. This can be brief for we shall meet specific examples of his interpretation in chapter five. Believing that "all serious [medieval] poetry" is allegorical unless it explicitly states "the message of charity", he asserts that confining oneself "to what a text 'actually says'" may be regarded by the historical critic, "not as a virtue but as a mark of illiteracy".[15] In *Fruyt and Chaf* Robertson and Huppé applied those principles in reading Chaucer and the result drew this protest from D. S. Brewer: "[Robertson and Huppé] deny the value of literature continually . . . since words do not mean what they say, and context is irrelevant, there can be no literary effect, and the authors are as hostile to the actuality of literature as any medieval exegete or scholastic." Before Brewer made this criticism M. W. Bloomfield had also complained that a poem "cannot normally have more meanings than what it says".[16] Robertson is being accused of writing his own poems to replace the actual texts he pretends to interpret. If the accusation is correct, Robertson's case disintegrates. However, Robertson himself has said that "a sign is controlled by its context."[17] Unfortunately he does not work out the relationship between this statement and the assertion that confining oneself to what a text "actually says" may be "a mark of illiteracy". This

---

[14] For example, Bloomfield, "Symbolism in Medieval Literature", M. *Phil*, 56 (1958), 73. It is more than coincidence that fourteen years previously Auerbach's figural approach, based on the rigid separation of Judaeo-Christian typology from hellenistic allegory, was also stimulated by irritation with certain other literary pan-allegorists (see his essay on "Figura" in *Scenes from the Drama of European Literature* (New York, 1959, 68).

[15] *Preface*, 287.

[16] Brewer, RES, 16 (1965), 305; Bloomfield, M. *Phil*, 56 (1958), 74 ff; see also reviews by J. Misrahi, R *Phil*, 17 (1964), 555–69; W. Matthews, R *Phil*, 17 (1964), 634–43; F. L. Utley, R *Phil*, 19 (1965), 250–60; R. O. Payne, CL, 15 (1963), 269–76.

[17] *Preface*, 298.

omission is a grave weakness in his position, and even the sympathetic R. E. Kaske admits that despite the bulk of *A Preface to Chaucer* a fundamental problem remains unexamined: "What kind of relationships are possible between the literal and the extra-literal meanings in literary allegory...?"[18] Robertson's only critical model for facing this problem may be called "the shell and kernel" model: figurative expression conceals a discursive kernel of truth which is always "a truth already familiar in other forms", always "something already known", while the figurative expression is a shell which exists purely as an enticing "puzzle".[19] Most literary critics find such views of figurative language totally inadequate, but instead of pursuing the point here it will suffice to recall a paragraph from Wittgenstein's *Philosophical Investigations*:

> We speak of understanding a sentence in the sense in which it can be replaced by another which says the same; but also in the sense in which it cannot be replaced by another. (Any more than one musical theme can be replaced by another.)

> In the one case the thought in the sentence is something common to different sentences; in the other, something that is expressed only by these words in these positions. (Understanding a poem.)[20]

Literary critics should be acutely conscious of the latter sense, and should be fully engaged with it. But it is just here that Robertson has proved unresponsive.

Turning to Robertson's opponents we find that they have been eclectic in their tactics. Despite claiming that Scriptural interpretation and poetics are utterly separate, they have not hesitated to draw arguments from exegetical theory in the hope of discrediting Robertson's approach to literature. They have stressed the "theological commonplace" that Christianity is a religion committed to history and the Bible's literal sense, what the text "actually says" in Robertson's terms. As an example of the opposition to Robertson, we can take a popular essay on those problems by C. Donahue.[21] Resting his case on the familiar polarization of Judaeo-Christian and hellen-

---

[18] I write "even" because, unlike Brewer or Bloomfield, Kaske states without demonstration, that Robertson's understanding of medieval Biblical exegesis proves that his method does not destroy a work's "concrete significance": see his review article, *ELH*, 30 (1963), 177; the quotation comes from 192.

[19] *Preface*, 32–3, 54; see also 55–6.

[20] *Philosophical Investigations*, tr. G. E. M. Anscombe (Oxford, 1968), I.531 (143–4).

[21] "Patristic Exegesis in the Criticism of Medieval Literature: The Summation", in *Critical Approaches to Medieval Literature*, ed. D. Bethurum (New York, 1960); his essay henceforward cited as Donahue.

istic culture, he makes a simple separation between figurative procedures which stem from the former and are "typological" and those
which come from the latter and are "allegorical". For instance, he
states that "the main bent" of St Augustine's exegesis "is 'Hebraic',
typological, rather than allegorical in the Greek sense." This
"'Hebraic', typological" tradition is "very insistent on the fundamental character of the historical reading" and is the dominant
medieval one. Although he uses the theory which separates exegesis
from poetics ("there is no question of a literary method . . ."),
Donahue claims that "the typological method of Christian exegesis
might turn imaginative writers towards realism rather than allegory."[22]
He is thus at one with Robertson in believing that exegesis exerted an
"influence" on literature though he strongly disagrees about the
nature of exegesis and the nature of its "influence". However, it
cannot be too strongly emphasized that Donahue does not undertake
any close reading of actual exegetical practice to support his assertions. The kind of response his work has evoked in some critics may
be illustrated by T. P. Dunning's acclaim of Donahue's "superb and
satisfying analysis of what patristic and medieval exegesis is: a
constant and unwavering preoccupation with the literal sense: and an
appreciation of a further typological rather than an allegorical
meaning".[23] It is rather surprising that an article without one example
of medieval exegetical practice should be called a "superb and
satisfying *analysis* of what patristic and medieval exegesis is"; it is as
strange that an article which contains no close reading of exegesis
could be accepted as having demonstrated what the "preoccupation"
of exegesis was in practice. But the fact that such an eminent scholar
as Dunning offers this enthusiastic and unexamined accolade,
suggests that the subject is indeed

> A gulf profound as that Serbonian bog
> Betwixt Damiata and Mount Casius old,
> Where armies whole have sunk . . .
> *Paradise Lost* II.592–4

The crucial omission of any close reading of actual exegetical practice is characteristic of the "opposition", and it prompts a reader to
wonder why critics should centre a case on exegesis when they have
no intention of examining it. The answer to this, I think, lies in the
impact of Robertson's work on medieval studies. Claiming to
represent genuine "historical criticism" he seemed to return allegory
to the old definition which once brought it into disrepute, a definition
usually phrased in terms like these: "When one thing is told, and by
that another is understood", which so easily becomes "the A = B

---

[22] Donahue, 62–7, 72–5 and see 77–9, 81.
[23] Dunning, *RES*, 14 (1963), 283.

equation basic to allegory".[24] Against this the opposition wished to argue that figurative writing was as "unparaphrasable" as other poetic language.[25] Feeling their case would be much strengthened by meeting Robertson's "historical criticism" on its own ground, they appealed to medieval exegesis. One of the more recent examples of such attempts is Rosemond Tuve's:

> It seems to me that these long centuries of practice and acceptance of Christian allegorical interpretation left a mark on the ordinary understanding of allegory. The more so because careful theory, New Testament sanction and doctrinally necessary safeguards helped to keep the recognized definition of allegory incredibly pure.[26]

Here is the usual conflation of theory and practice. Like other scholars, she omits any analysis of actual exegetical practice while insisting that the "incredibly pure" definition of allegory meant that throughout the Middle Ages, "there is no question of a substitution of figurative for literal meaning."[27] This claim is central in the opposition's polemic, but it is all too apparent that polemic is no substitute for concrete analysis.

Another example of the opposition's approach is M. W. Bloomfield's attack on modern allegorical critics. He objects that their activities are an "attempt to systematize" the four levels of medieval exegesis, and this "can lead only to a debased and mechanical interpretation of the highest mysteries. Such attempts reveal a profound misunderstanding of all historical study."[28] The methods Bloomfield depicts might well lead to "a debased and mechanical interpretation of the highest mysteries", but there is absolutely no *a priori* reason to assume that "such attempts" were *not* made by medieval writers. The problem here, of course, is to establish whether "such attempts" *were* made, and if they were, in what forms and with what effects. It

---

[24] John Harrington in *Elizabethan Critical Essays*, ed. G. G. Smith (London, 1967), 11.202; K. Stone, *Middle English Prose Style* (The Hague, 1970), 81; see too J. B. Allen, *The Friar as Critic* (Nasheville, 1971), 6–8. The results of such assumptions are amusingly illustrated in the Variorum Spenser, *The Works of Edmund Spenser*, ed. E. Greenlaw *et al.*, 10 vols. (Baltimore, 1932–57), for example I.431, 447, 460.

[25] For example, C. S. Lewis, *The Allegory of Love* (London, 1958), 124–5; H. Berger, *The Allegorical Temper* (New Haven 1957), 166; A. C. Hamilton, *The Structure of Allegory in the Faerie Queene* (London, 1961), 11, 12, 17, 29; T. P. Roche, *The Kindly Flame* (Princeton, 1964), 31.

[26] *Allegorical Imagery* (Princeton, 1966), 44–8, 223, 413–51, see too 47–8, 403, 430–1.

[27] *Allegorical Imagery*, 222 and note on same page.

[28] Bloomfield, *M Phil*, 56 (1958), 76: but it is interesting that Robertson himself warns against attempts to systematize here, *Preface*, 298–9.

is typical of the whole controversy that Bloomfield himself offers no analysis of the practice of figurative writing in homiletics or exegesis.

Frequently critics take "typology" and "allegory" as distinct classes of writing and (as we saw with Donahue) the former is aligned with Judaeo-Christian historicity and realism, the later with a hellenistic-platonic flight from history. This move, however, involves difficulties which are serious enough to discredit it, and I shall now show why this is so, beginning with one of the most influential proponents of the "rigorous distinction between typology and allegory", J. Daniélou. He maintains that they are "opposites" and states that allegory is "closely connected with the religious atmosphere of the hellenistic world", whereas typology is the true Judaeo-Christian inheritance. While allegory dissolves history into timeless generalities, in typology "there is a correspondence between historical realities at different stages in sacred history."[29] This argument springs from the "theological commonplace" already discussed, and clearly, in such a confused field as criticism of medieval allegorical literature nothing could be more welcome than a "rigorous distinction". In fact, Daniélou's work has been embraced by many critics, and is so well known that there is no need to summarize its features any further.[30]

But this separation is much more problematic than Daniélou's work allows. Theologians themselves are neither unanimous about the "rigorous distinction", nor are they agreed as to precisely what constitutes hellenistic allegory and what constitutes specifically Christian allegorical (or typological) interpretation and writing. Although this important complication is rarely acknowledged by literary critics intent on appealing to a medieval "typological" tradition with which they can discredit modern "allegorical" readers like Robertson, it is easy to illustrate. For instance, in an attempt to demonstrate the hellenizing traits of Origen's exegesis, R. P. C. Hanson not only differs strongly from de Lubac in his assessment, but finds Daniélou's "rigorous distinction" inadequate.[31] While he acclaims Daniélou's "masterly analysis of early Christian typology", he can still classify a piece of Origen's exegesis as "Philonic", hellenistic allegory, although to Daniélou it seemed genuine

[29] Daniélou, *Origen*, tr. W. Mitchell (London, 1955), 327 n. 2; see chapter three in that book and also: "The Fathers and the Scriptures", *Theology*, 57 (1954), 83–9; "The Conception of History in the Christian Tradition", *JR*, 30 (1950), 171–9; "The Problem of Symbolism", *Thought*, 25 (1950), 423–40; *From Shadows to Reality*, tr. W. Hibberd (London, 1960).

[30] Used by such critics as: B. K. Lewalski, *Milton's Brief Epic* (London, 1966), 168–9; W. G. Madsen, *From Shadowy Types to Truth* (New Haven, 1968); Elizabeth Salter, "Medieval Poetry and the Figural View of Reality", *PBA*, 54 (1968), 76 and note; V. A. Kolve, *The Play Called Corpus Christi* (London, 1966), chapter four; R. B. Burlin, *The Old English Advent: A Typological Approach* (New Haven, 1968), chapter one.

[31] R. P. C. Hanson, *Allegory and Event* (London, 1959), see 123–9, 204–7, 249–50 and 250 n. 6.

Christian, "typology". Furthermore, he challenges Daniélou's analysis of the way Origen reads the conflict between Jacob and Esau in Genesis. Daniélou judged Origen's exegesis "authentic typology", but Hanson argues that this is unconvincing since, in his opinion, Origen has made a "step into the non-historical world of Hellenistic allegory", a step taken "with the aid of Philonic exegesis".[32] Similarly, when A. C. Charity attempts to assess the relationship between hermeneutical practice and a text's own challenge, he decides that much of what Daniélou accepted as authentic typology is "somewhat wooden, a mechanical game of contrivance".[33]

Such characteristic disagreements between scholars of typology should deter literary critics from making simple statements about the existence of two easily separable traditions, one hellenistic and allegorical, one Judaeo-Christian and typological. (Typical of the manifold complexities in this area is the fact that allegory was native to Palestine.[34]) These differences of opinion assure us that we have no reason to take the terms "allegory" and "typology" as clearly distinct categories. Too easily they become persuasive definitions in a circular polemic carried on at a safe distance from the actual practices of medieval figurative work.[35]

To reinforce this claim I shall now discuss some positions taken up by critics in which the supposed "rigorous distinction" between typology and allegory has encouraged the evasion of real problems and the perpetuation of confusion. In a book on *Pearl*, I. Bishop calls medieval exegesis typological and claims that its historical focus separates it unequivocally from "the system of the Platonists that regards the phenomena of the world as mere shadows and imperfect copies of the reality of an archetypal world of ideas". Like others, Bishop finds that exegetical methods were employed by poets in commentaries on their own works or those of other secular authors. He cites Boccaccio who uses "the fourfold method in his exposition of myth" in the *De Genealogia*.[36] But if "typological" reading handles sacred history in the way Boccaccio handles pagan myth, then the rigorous separation of non-Christian symbolical methods from

---

[32] *Allegory and Event*, 252–3; dissent recurs, e.g., 281–3, 353–6.
[33] A. C. Charity, *Events and their Afterlife: The Dialectics of Christian Typology in the Bible and Dante* (Cambridge, 1966) 58; see his Introduction, Parts I and II, especially 177–8, 204–7, 258–9.
[34] J. Bonsirven, *Exégèse Rabbinique et Exégèse Paulienne* (Paris, 1938), chapters I, II, IV and especially 74–6, 207–41, 246–9, 308–11; confirmed in Hanson, *Allegory and Event*, chapter I and 89.
[35] Similar warnings come from the theologian J. Barr, *Old and New in Interpretation* (London, 1966), 104–5; also relevant here his *Biblical Words for Time* (New York, 1962), 137 and chapters II–IV, VI, and T. Boman, *Hebrew Thought Compared with Greek*, tr. J. L. Moreau (London, 1960), 125–6, 142–3, 193.
[36] *Pearl in its Setting* (Oxford, 1968), 51–5 (the sentence about the Platonists is on 55), 137 n. 1, 138 n. 14.

Christian ones seems quite meaningless. For an example of Boccaccio's exegesis we can take his interpretation of the Prometheus myth
(IV.44). First he handles it euhemeristically (although Biblical
exegesis eschewed euhemerism); then he says that figuratively
Prometheus is God the Creator, Nature or prelapsarian Adam. The
second Prometheus is the learned man teaching, the fire stolen from
the Sun's chariot-wheel is the gleam of Truth proceeding from God
which lights everyone who is in the world; the wheel itself symbolizes
eternity. Prometheus' "furtive method hints that truth is not to be
found in crowded cities but only by meditation in silent solitudes".[37]
This figural method turns myth into banal generalizations about
truth and cities, while imagistic context and allegorical "kernel"
neither interact nor interrelate. The images are taken as models
from which various sets of informative statements can be decoded. It
is the kind of exegesis for which Robertson and Huppé have been
attacked, and it is *against* such methods that literary critics have often
appealed to the practice and influence of Biblical exegesis, which
Bishop himself calls "typological". But if, as Bishop also seems to
hold, the methods of Christian exegesis are the same as Boccaccio's,
then the critics' appeal to exegesis serves no purpose. Once again, it is
not even clear on what grounds the practice of Christian allegory is
being separated from the practice of non-Christian allegory. It may
be pointed out that Bishop does not himself see the need to examine
any Biblical exegesis, and here I believe the terms "typology" and
"allegory", being used as distinct categories, have played their part
in concealing this need.

A critic who has laid great weight on the difference between the
theologians' allegory (what others call typology) and the poets'
allegory is C. S. Singleton. He attacked the allegory of the poets as "a
false way", one which no "poet of rectitude" could possibly use
because its "first meaning was a disembodied fiction". In a later
article he appealed to "the whole exegetical tradition" in support of
his distinctions.[38] Here he was responding to R. H. Green's insistence
that "the literal sense of the *Divine Comedy* is a poet's fiction" and its
figurative mode that used in Alan of Lille's allegorical visions. The
mode, according to Green, is adequately described by Boccaccio:

There have been, and still are, many of our own Christian poets,
who beneath the covering of their fictions [sub tegminibus

---

[37] *On Poetry, Being the Preface and the Fourteenth and Fifteenth Books of
Boccaccio's Genealogia Deorum Gentilium*, tr. with introductory essay, C. G.
Osgood (Princeton, 1930), xxiiiff.
[38] Singleton, "Dante's Allegory", *Spec*, 25 (1950), 78–86, and "The
Irreducible Dove", *CL*., 9 (1957), 129–35; see R. Hollander, *Allegory in Dante's
Commedia* (Princeton, 1969), for a development of Singleton position.

fictionum suarum], have set forth the sacred truths of the Christian religion. And to choose one example among many, our Dante. . . .

Singleton contradicts Boccaccio and Green, stating that Dante's allegory is an "imitation of God's way of writing" as understood by "the whole exegetical tradition".[39] These assertions and counter-assertions are not entirely trivial, since the question at issue is how we should approach the poem. Are we to read it as Boccaccio reads classical mythology, and as Green advises? What kind of interpretation is relevant? But Singleton's appeal to "the whole exegetical tradition" rashly takes at least one central point for granted: that the practice of allegory in exegesis coincides with his idea of its figural theory. If it were to be shown that "God's way of writing", despite Christianity's historical commitment was not understood in the way Singleton assumes, but in a manner close to "the poets' allegory", then his appeal to "the whole exegetical tradition" would not serve his intention at all. Furthermore, there are questions about the theory of exegesis which are not asked: were medieval views of history and image entirely free from hellenistic, especially neo-platonic notions? If not, what effects did these have? In Robertson's opinion Christian allegory reduced time and history to "a kind of continuous presence", and we have now seen how his opponents, deploying the category "typology" (or "allegory of the theologians"), hold an antithetical view of medieval figura.[40] Once more we draw the moral that the issues raised cannot be resolved while critics make appeals to doctrinal theory and terms like "typology" in place of close analysis of actual allegorical practices. Since the terms allegory and typology are extremely tricky if taken as distinct categories, the onus is definitely on each individual literary critic to *show* what kind of writing he is characterizing, and to show how it handles history, idea and image. Here specific literary analysis is essential, for only out of this will relevant distinctions and interpretations emerge. Failure can only ensure the eternal return of the contradictory appeals to the same exegetical tradition, turning the study of medieval allegory into a critical limbo.

The situation just outlined suggests that the analysis of medieval figurative writing might be helped by some critical terms which are not utterly dependent on unexamined assumptions about Biblical exegesis and the medieval practice of "typology". Vocabulary based

---

[39] For R. H. Green, see "Dante's Allegory of Poets and the Medieval Theory of Poetic Fiction", CL, 9 (1957), 118–28; for his practice, "Alan of Lille's *De Planctu Naturae*", Spec, 31 (1956), 649–74; for Singleton's disagreement, CL, 9 (1957), 132–3.
[40] For a recent interesting statement of the "opposition" approach, see Elizabeth Salter, "Medieval Poetry and the Figural View of Reality", PBA, 54 (1968), 73–92.

on unexamined assumptions beguiles the critic into believing that the
necessary work has been done when, in fact, it quite simply hasn't.
With this danger in mind I have avoided using the terms "allegory"
and "typology" as though they are distinct and proven critical categories. I use these terms when the kind of writing they are designa-
ting has been made clear in concrete analysis. On a number of
occasions, especially in the last three chapters, I have borrowed some
vocabulary from I. T. Ramsey's studies in theological language, the
terms "disclosure model", "picture model" and "read off", which
occur in conjunction and are discussed. Ramsey sees theological
discourse as an attempt to be articulate about an insight into structure
and patterns of existential and universal significance, an insight which
he calls a "cosmic disclosure". The religious writer wishing to communicate his insight relies on various models from which he hopes
the "cosmic disclosure" may be generated for his reader, "and in
terms of which we are articulate about what those disclosures
disclose". But a "picture model" is taken as one from which the
reader can, or believes he can, "read off discourse from it without let
or hindrance", as in technological scale models. Ramsey argues that
theological insights cannot satisfactorily use "a scale or picture
model" and he insists that confusion of "picture models" with
theological "disclosure models" has led to some of the most disastrous pieces of Christian theology.[41] The function of these terms in
particular pieces of analysis will make the meaning they have in my
own study explicit enough: where they are used they are used as aids
to help us discriminate between different kinds of figurative writing
which in turn ask for different kinds of figurative reading.

I must, however, make it clear that my own use of Ramsey's work
does not imply full sympathy with his overall attempt to defend
orthodox piety from the sceptical attacks of modern analytic/
empirical philosophy. (He hoped to associate this challenge with
simple misconceptions about the nature of theological language and
in doing so he developed the distinctions between models just outlined.) The justification for applying Ramsey's terms in parts of my
book is that they help to distinguish between figurative modes and
models employed within a traditional Catholic framework long
before Ramsey's encounter with British philosophy had been dreamed
of. The writers I deal with here are all orthodox Christians and
Ramsey's work helps us to see that when they give us "picture
models" they are not doing so because they have any wish to subvert
traditional orthodoxies and conventional habits of belief and action:
as we shall see, their use of "picture models" rests on confusions of

---

[41] Three relevant books by I. T. Ramsey, *Religious Language* (London, 1957);
Models and Mystery (London, 1964); *Christian Discourse* (London, 1965); see too
M. Black, *Models and Metaphors* (New York, 1962), chapters III and XIII.

2 Christian Allegory

Ideas cannot be Given but in their minutely Appropriate Execution.

Blake, *Public Address*

I

So far I have accepted that the "theological commonplace" stressing Christianity's firm commitment to history was as normal to medieval as to modern theology. But before undertaking a critique of medieval figural practices I wish to make some qualifications to this commonplace. These qualifications will not deny the importance of the "theological commonplace" to the Christian dialectic and its claims—I have already pointed out that the key to the theory of Christian allegory was taken to be the historical Incarnation of God, and we recall Augustine's complaint that however much he learnt about the eternal Word from the Platonists he never found, "and the Word was made flesh, and dwelt among us."[1] Nevertheless, discussing modern emphasis on Christianity's historical foundation, McIntyre offers a warning:

> What is not always realised is that historical conceptions of this sort are unique to our time; that because of developments not only in theological thought concerning the subjects peculiar to itself but also in the fields of historical methodology and the critique of historiography, our understanding of our interpretation of the historical element in the Christian faith are not the same as those of any previous generation.[2]

Others have commented on divergences between medieval and modern hermeneutics in this context, and it is the relevance of some divergences to our subject that we will now notice.[3]

---

[1] *Confessions*, VII.9.
[2] J. McIntyre, *The Christian Doctrine of History* (Edinburgh, 1957), 3.
[3] Those requiring fuller documentation than I intend to offer in this section may consult my D.Phil. thesis, "Allegorical Modes: A Critical Study with special reference to Piers Plowman" (in University of York library, 1971), chapter two, section two and notes.

In an essay on symbolic theology and scholastic exegesis M-D. Chenu argued that medieval culture inherited a situation where the Bible and Christianity had been "blocked up by the categories of hellenistic culture deployed by Philo and Origen". He was convinced that the practice of medieval exegesis reflected this situation and explored the way historical specificity and the actions of men are dissolved, while the narrative becomes an occasion for constructing archetypes and universals. He attributed this process explicitly to the effects of Platonism and as a modern theologian found it incongruous with the historicity of Christianity.[4]

Considering early Christian exegesis J. N. D. Kelly reached similar conclusions. Kelly discovered that the Latin Fathers reveal an "unhistorical approach" which failed to grapple with the particularity of events and people, so that although *The City of God* takes history as the field of God's self-disclosure, Augustine "made little or no attempt to link these reflexions with his elucidation of the biblical message". At the root of the Christian exegetical tradition there thus seems to be a "failure to appreciate the significance of history, in particular its significance as the arena of God's progressive revelation". This failure is associated with a "too mechanical conception of inspiration", and "the fatal corollary of the absolute inerrancy of Scripture in all its parts". The consequences are that:

> instead of frankly accepting the fact that the divine message was conveyed in earthen vessels and that God's activity and purpose can be discerned in events sometimes apparently trivial, they felt entitled, even obliged, to find the chief significance of much of the Bible in allegories and spiritual or mystical interpretation which were at best ingenious readings back into it of the accepted Christian ideas, and at worst entirely subjective fancies.[5]

However much this may surprise critics who have stressed the "Hebraic" and "typological" nature of Christian exegesis, we shall find Kelly's conclusions well based.

Such qualifications to the "theological commonplace" from which we started are strengthened by other studies. In examining St Augustine's exegesis M. Pontet shows how often Augustine neglects the temporal aspects of the phenomena he is handling, even making figural correspondences "verbal rather than historical". In one of the typical examples he offers Augustine connects the fig tree of

---

[4] "Théologie Symbolique et Exégèse Scolastique aux XIIᵉ–XIIIᵉ siècles", in *Mélanges J. de Ghellinck* (Gembloux; 1951), 525–6; Chenu, "*Involucrum*: Le Mythe selon les théologiens médiévaux", *AHDLMA*, 22 (1955), 79.

[5] "The Bible and the Latin Fathers", in *The Church's Use of the Bible, Past and Present*, ed. D. Nineham (London, 1963), 41–56, here especially 53–4.

John 1.48 with the forbidden tree of Genesis 2 and 3. In John 1.48 Jesus tells Nathaniel that before Philip called him, "when thou wast under the fig tree, I saw thee." Here Augustine not only detects a figural reference to the fall, but states that Nathaniel represents "all mankind". Pontet contends that the effect of such allegory is the virtual suppression of history and a flight from its windings and contingencies. Augustine destroys contexts and, Pontet concludes that his spirituality did not find it congenial to localize the figural revelation of Scriptures.[6] Another interesting discussion of medieval exegesis, by a modern theologian, occurs in G. W. H. Lampe's essay on Biblical typology. Lampe notes that patristic and medieval exegetes refer to "the letter which kills" and "the spirit" of St Paul as the literal and the allegoric senses.[7] He argues that this approach "rests, not on an interpretation of history but on a particular quasi-Platonist doctrine of the literal sense of Scripture—the outward form or 'letter' of the sacred writings—to the eternal spiritual reality concealed, as it were, beneath the literal sense". The Bible was "a mysterious collection of enigmas" and history became "the outward shell or husk containing and hiding from the uninstructed the inner truth of the mystery". Lampe thinks these beliefs stemmed from Philo and dominated the whole western tradition. This tradition's figura,

> must be referred to Hellenistic ideas about the correspondence of the earthly order as the shadow with the intelligible sphere as the reality, to the Alexandrian tradition of moralising allegorisation of the Homeric poems, and to a lesser extent to Rabbinic exegesis with its disregards of the context and the original meaning of proof-text. Hebranic and Greek elements are intertwined in allegorical texts.[8]

It is useful to be reminded that hellenistic elements were important components of Christian tradition, and Lampe develops his own attack against "the allegory of the theologians" on the ground that its methods were "wholly unhistorical".[9] This is a crucial challenge to the assumptions of literary critics following Auerbach and Donahue, as is the overwhelming presence of "the erroneous Origen" in the Western exegetical tradition. Beryl Smalley, having aligned

---

[6] *L'Exégèse de St. Augustin Prédicateur* (Paris, 1946), 131, 153, 163, 166, 333 ff., 582–4.

[7] Another commplace, see illustration in de Lubac, *Exégèse*, I.2. 440–8; II.1.199–209; II. 1.101–436 *passim*; II. 2.60–72, 81–3, 94–6, 271, 274, 306 n. 4, 315–16.

[8] G. W. H. Lampe and K. J. Woolcombe, *Essays in Typology* (London 1957), 21, 30, 32.

[9] Lampe, *ibid*, 33–8: on hellenistic models incorporated in Christian theology see brief comments by Ramsey, *Christian Discourse*, 20–1. Substantiating Lampe's case, see A. Richardson, *History Sacred and Profane* (London, 1962), 75–9. A most fruitful approach here might be to follow H. Descroche, *Marxisme et Religions* (Paris, 1962), 54–64.

Origen's allegorical modes with Philo's, remarks "to write a history of Origenist influence on the west would be tantamount to writing a history of western exegesis." The accuracy of this statement has been fully demonstrated by de Lubac, who shows how Origen's exegesis was absorbed into standard medieval allegory.[10] We will meet an example of Origen's allegory in the next section but it is worth recalling how Hanson, after assembling a mass of Origen's figurative practices, argued that "in history as event, in history as the field of God's self-revelation *par excellence*, Origen is not in the least interested. He is only interested in history as parable."[11] We see how little reason there is to *assume* that medieval figurative practice will necessarily manifest the traits Auerbach and Donahue ascribed to "typology", with its "Hebraic" emphasis on historical process and events. Free from such presuppositions the results of my own analysis of exegetical *figura* and related allegory should be less surprising.

One further aspect of the qualifications I am making should be mentioned, however briefly. It involves the way images were viewed whether drawn from the Bible or nature, the way "it became accepted that creation itself is an allegorical book revealing beneath the 'literal' or visible surface of objects 'the invisible things of God' (Romans 1.20)." This use of Romans 1.20 was common in early exegetical theory, and it seems to have connections with neoplatonic thought, connections which would reinforce the qualifications already made about medieval handling of history and event in allegory.[12] Certainly, when Macrobius, one of the most widely read authors of the Middle Ages, asserted that the visible things of nature act as mirrors of the higher and incorporeal world, he expressed a basic tenet of neoplatonic theology.[13] This alerts us to some interesting implications in the medieval belief that Christian allegory generates meaning in the same way as nature-symbolism. Let us again recollect the customary contrast between Judaeo-Christian historicity and non-Christian naturalizing of history: in *Piers Plowman as a Fourteenth Century Apocalypse*, M. W. Bloomfield reiterates that "the ancient Greeks and Romans" managed history by "reducing it to

---

[10] *Exégèse*, I.1.172–304 (*passim* but especially 211–19, 221–38, 240–4, 294–304); I.1.375–96, 415; I.2.538–46, 586–99; II.2.61, 155–62, 308: despite doubts about Origen's errors this remained true, *Exégèse*, I.1.245–50, 255, 257–90. For Beryl Smalley's statement, *The Study of the Bible in the Middle Ages* (Indiana, 1964), 14.

[11] *Allegory and Event* (London, 1959), 275–6; see also chapters V, X, 132–374 *passim*.

[12] Quotation from D. W. Robertson, *Preface to Chaucer*, 296, and see chapters II, and IV; see Huppé and Robertson, *Fruyt and Chaf* (Princeton, 1963), 7–8, 24; early examples include Origen, *Against Celsus*, III.47; Augustine's *Confessions*, V.1; VII.10, 17, 20 etc. For a contrasting approach, G. Josipovici, *The World and the Book* (London, 1973), 48 ff.

[13] *Commentary on the Dream of Scipio*, tr. W. H. Stahl (New York, 1952), I.14; on his popularity, introduction, 39–55. For Plotinus's version, *The Enneads*, II.9.16–18; in the Bible there was The Book of Wisdom, 13.1, 5.

nature", whereas "in the Christian tradition, following the Hebraic emphasis", history reveals religious truth and God's will.[14] However, if the Bible's events and images function like nature's unhistorical images, then Christian allegory, disclosed through sacred history, shares the same figurative mode as nature-symbolism and the poets' allegory. And if this is so, then once more we are led to ask, where lies the unique role of history and event in Christian allegory?

The answer seems to be that it was in great danger of vanishing; as in all spheres of figurative work symbolism supposedly based on historical events and processes was incorporated into an anti-historical nature-symbolism, shared by Philonic and hellenistic allegorical modes.[15] This answer is relevant to later medieval practice (as the next section of this chapter illustrates[16]) but it is now appropriate to sum up the balance reached so far between the "theological commonplace" of Christianity's historical commitment and my qualifications regarding medieval approaches to the role of history and image in generating allegorical meaning. It is true that medieval theory saw God's historical Incarnation as the key to Christian allegory.[17] Nevertheless, we have discovered models which qualify this Christocentric approach to a historically based symbolism. These qualifiers should prevent critics from absorbing medieval exegesis into any straightforward "typological", "Hebraic" paradigm. In fact, "hellenistic" conceptions of the relations between image and idea were prevalent—prevalent enough to draw adverse criticism from modern theologians for encouraging medieval exegesis to dissolve the historical engagement of Biblical *figura*. The tendency to assume that sacred history contains allegorical meaning in the same way as the unhistorical images of nature, implies that the unique Christian allegory (typology) may not be any different in practice from other kinds of allegory. We can hardly be amazed if nothing in medieval practice corresponds neatly to that "rigorous distinction" between Hebraic-Christian typology and hellenistic-Philonic allegory. Thus prepared, we can now move to the rather more concrete task of examining allegorical practices in detail.

---

[14] *Piers Plowman* (New Brunswick, 1961), 100–1.
[15] J. Chydenius, "The Theory of Medieval Symbolism", *CHL*, 27 (1960), 1–42, especially here 9–19: for corroboration, E. de Bruyne, *Etudes Médiévale Esthetique*, 3 vols. (Brussels, 1946), I.191–2, 342; II.200, 205, 208, 211, 220–4 etc.
[16] As pointed out in note three above, I have provided further discussion and documentation elsewhere, but it's worth noting the massive influence of pseudo-Dionysius on the later Middle Ages and the nature of his symbolic theory and practice: de Lubac, *Exégèse*, II.2.487–94 and R. Roques, *L'Univers Dionysien* (Paris, 1954), 53–4, 122–3 and chapter II.
[17] For example, St Bernard, *P. Lat.* 183.133; Hugh of St Victor *De Arca Morali*, II. 8; de Lubac, *Exégèse*, I.1.318–55.

II

The story of Rahab and the fall of Jericho (Joshua 2 and 6) is an especially appropriate place to begin since Auerbach has written an article in which the exegetes' treatment of this text is offered as an example of "typological treatment" in contrast to "allegorical symbolism". As usual he insists that the "important difference" between these two traditions is that in the former (illustrated by the standard exegesis of Rahab's history) "both the signifying and the signified facts are real and concrete historical events", whereas in the latter one of the two terms "is a pure sign". The "typological treatment" is the one representative of western tradition, "[where] neither the prefiguring nor the prefigured event lose their literal and historical reality by their figurative meaning and interrelation. This is a very important point."[18] As we have seen, it is certainly a very popular point, and one bristling with problems. Interpretations of this text can thus serve not only as representative examples of exegesis in the western tradition but also to put the claims of Auerbach and his followers to a practical test. But before the analysis I must again make it clear that such terms as "real and concrete" and "historical reality" are not given content simply by protestations of belief in a story's truth. Belief that an event was historically "real" can tell the reader nothing about the way it has been taken to generate allegorical meaning. Only a careful literary analysis of the actual expression should allow a reader to make Auerbach's kind of claim about exegesis.

In the Book of Joshua we read how Joshua sent out two spies to explore the land secretly (2.1). These two men enter the house of Rahab, a prostitute in Jericho. They are seen and reported to the King of Jericho. The ensuing narrative gives a detailed and particular description of Rahab deceiving the King's messengers, her initiative, her concealment of the scouts, her management of their hurried escape (2.2–24). In return for this aid she and her household are to be spared, *unless* she reports the scouts. Her house is to be identified by the scarlet cord which she used to let the spies escape out of her window. Daniélou has shown that many early exegetes practised what he calls "the typology of Rahab", and we can take Irenaeus as representative. This "typology" involves turning the two scouts into three and then stating, "which three were doubtless the Father, Son and the Holy Spirit". The typologist also claims that "Rahab and all her house were preserved through faith in the scarlet sign." The first of these figurations needed an obvious adjustment of the narrative

---

[18] "Typological Symbolism in Medieval Literature", *Yale French Review*, 9 (1952), 3–10, see p. 6.

itself; it also required neglect of the narrative's context. For instance, who "sent" the Trinity? The history's concrete details—the dialogue about hiding, the escape and flight, Rahab's life or death pledge to silence—are also ignored. The second figuration, connecting the cord with the Exodus and Redemption, is well known.[19] This too demands an adjustment to the narrative if the exegete is to find the decisions of Christian dogmatics concealed in the image. But this approach does not simply coincide with Auerbach's statements about the exegetes' stress on "historical reality" in their *figura*. For Rahab is not primarily saved through a religious "faith": *she* in fact took the initiative and *she* struck the bargain with the two spies (in Irenaeus' typology, the Trinity). She did indeed have a shrewd prudential kind of "faith", in that she believed it would be senseless to resist an invading army which had already revealed its irresistibility through its supernatural supporter (Joshua 2.4–13). These, then, are the causes of her salvation. The scarlet cord plays an extremely minor and external role in her preservation, for it is simply a sign for recognition. Placing this so centrally in the figural reading of the narrative tends both to distort the narrative's movement and to do less than justice to the unique centrality of the acts of Redemption in the theology of man's salvation.

Irenaeus does not develop this allegory ("typology") much further, but Origen does, and his expansion guides medieval exegesis of the text. Although the relevant passage from his third homily on Joshua has been discussed by Daniélou, I shall summarize his figurative interpretation. Unlike Irenaeus, Origen thinks the two scouts are an image of the angels. As for Rahab, etymology can reveal her significance before any attention is paid to the historical narrative's generation of meaning: Rahab means *latitudo*, and "what is this breath, save the Church of Christ which is made up of sinners and harlots. It is this breath which receives the spies of Jesus (Joshua)." When Rahab advises the two scouts to hide in the mountains, Origen maintains that figuratively this conveys an idea: "She gives them mysterious and heavenly counsel, having nothing of the mundane in it; Go ye up to the mountains; that is to say, do not pass through the valleys, flee from base things, proclaim what is lofty and elevated." And when Rahab and the scouts agree on the scarlet cord as the sign of the bargain, Origen comments, "she did not take any other sign but the scarlet one, which has the appearance of blood. For she knew that there was no salvation for man save in the blood of Christ."[20] Origen then enlarges the bargain Rahab struck for herself and her

---

[19] Daniélou, *From Shadows to Reality* (London, 1960), 244 ff.; tr. in Ante-Nicene Christian Library (Edinburgh, 1868), 450–1.

[20] *From Shadows to Reality*, 249–51 (text in P.G. 12.839–60).

household, to take in anyone who enters Rahab's house. This has no warrant from the "historical reality". It arises because the inter-pretation of Rahab as the "Church" offering the scouts/angels heavenly counsel has so engulfed the primary events and text that they are ignored.

Again we notice that historical and literary context are unimpor-tant in the exegete's development of the text's significance. But instead of repeating comments already made about Irenaeus' "typology" I will look more closely at the way Origen understands Rahab's dealings with the scouts in Joshua 2. Far from "nothing of the mundane", the history gives us everything of the mundane (2.6–8; 12–22). Rahab's council is to flee pursuers and escape to the mountains, "lest perhaps they meet you as they return; and there lie ye hid three days, till they come back. And so you shall go on your way" (2.16). Later the scouts return to this land (2.18; 6.20–6). Rahab advises the scouts to hide, and Origen's "typology" takes this as advice to "proclaim" elevated sentiments. Any relation of image and idea to historical context is dissolved, and it does not seem that Auerbach's "historical reality" is of much consequence in Origen's understanding of the way images signify.

Because he takes the cord as the sign of the cross, Origen has to credit Rahab with the knowledge that there is no salvation except through the blood of Christ. But we should again note that it is Rahab who *initiates* the bargain by which she is saved, and she has no sense of sin or need of justification. She simply strikes a bargain, "swear . . . that as I have shewn mercy to you, so you also will shew mercy to my father's house" (2.12). The exegete wishes to include the doctrinal notion that salvation is God's initiative, but in reading the dogma from this context he has to dissolve the events and the accompanying images, in effect though not in "belief". The particular movements of the narrative and images have to be ignored. Other problems are raised by this way of reading but perhaps the most striking facet is the dissolution of history and the specificity of image in the allegory (or "typology").

Origen's interpretation entered the Western exegetical tradition and became standard. Daniélou follows it up to Gregory the Great, but the great *Glossa* incorporated and developed it. We are thus not surprised to find Nicholas of Lyra stating in the fourteenth century that the text shows Rahab thinking of her spiritual salvation as well as physical survival. His allegory proceeds in this way: the two scouts "are understood" as "disciples sent by Jesus Christ to preach through the world", while they also signify the two precepts of charity; Rahab's house, "that is, the gentiles"; the King of Jericho signifies the devil trying to exterminate the evangelical preachers, while the latter convert gentiles to Christ. (Compare Joshua 6.17–21!) In his allegory on Joshua 6 he adds that the scarlet cord expresses, "the cross of Christ, which is the sign of salvation".[21] On into the fifteenth century Denis the Carthusian still sees fit to open his commentary on the Book of Joshua by citing Origen himself as an authority for thinking that "this book does not so much relate to the actions of Joshua, son of Nun, as to the sacraments of our Lord Jesus." We are prepared for his allegory (or, "typology") of Joshua 2 and 6. The two scouts are read as "holy angels sent invisibly into the world", or as "holy preachers", or as the two Testaments. These readings are traditional enough. Rahab immediately receives the etymology "latitudo", though to Denis this designates, "the gentiles, who were spread throughout the world". The King of Jericho retains his status as Devil, and Denis also sees in him a figure for heretics and tyrants. In Joshua 2.6 Rahab took the two scouts (hardly made into invisible angels without ruthless allegorizing) onto the roof of her house to hide them with the stalks of flax which she had placed there. Denis explains the meaning of this incident: "The roof of the house is the devoted mind of the Church, or the mystical understanding of scripture, or ecclesiastical worth or the grace of contemplation." Rahab "is" the Church calling preachers to contemplation. This figuration does acknowledge Rahab's initiative in the historical narrative, but problems remain as knotty as before, and of the same kind. If Rahab, that is the church, hides her preachers on the roof, that is in contemplation of mystical understanding of the Bible, how is she converted by Christ's preacher's, which Denis also maintains? And what are we to make of the self-saving bargain she makes with the preachers/scouts/testaments/angels?[22] The images are removed from their controlling contexts and attached to certain terms of a different order, pell-mell. Again the time-dimension, so vital to the notion of progressive revelation, is destroyed. We recall how Auerbach insisted that traditional "typological treatment" of Joshua 2 and 6 emphasized "the real and concrete" nature of historical events in its figurations. In the light of my analysis it does not seem that his position can be maintained. Of course all these exegetes believed that the narrated events were "true" and "historical" and "real"; and of course they did not think they were dealing with myth. But this is just not to the point, for we are concerned with modes of expression and communication, and with doctrine only *in relation* to these. Nor is it to the point that in his literal column Nicholas of Lyra shows great interest in geography, history and chronology. For we will remember that our concern here is with *figura*, not with geography and chronology.

---

[21] *From Shadows to Reality*, 253–9; *Glossa* and Nicholas of Lyra printed in Nicholas of Lyra's *Postillae*, 6 vols. (Basil, 1506–8), here II.5B ff., and II.5D ff.. Same edition used throughout.
[22] Denis the Carthusian, *Ennarationes in V. et N. Testamenti Libros*, 8 vols. (Cologne, 1531–5), this edition used throughout, here II.3A, II.5A ff., 11E–12B.

Next I shall take a fairly well known piece of medieval exegesis. It is well known largely because it is strikingly paradoxical, but its importance in the current critique lies in the methods employed, for these are absolutely standard. The text is in 2 Kings (Samuel) 11, the story of David, his arrangements for killing Uriah and his adultery with Bath-Sheba. H. de Lubac cites over fifteen medieval exegetes who follow the standard interpretation I shall record. De Lubac calls the exegesis "subtle", but he emphasizes the normality of the principles on which it is based. Denis the Carthusian neatly summarizes the whole tradition in his commentary on the chapter. He refers his reader to the *Glossa* which explains how what appears evil in the historical narrative can in reality signify goodness. Then he says, "by David here Isidore understands [intelligit] Christ, by Uriah the devil, by Bath-Sheba the Church acquired from the gentiles." As David kills Uriah (arranged his death, actually), so Christ, "when the devil was conquered, joined to himself the church from the gentiles which the devil had possessed before". Denis also gives an alternative reading: here Uriah is understood as the Synagogue, Bath-Sheba as the Law, David still as Christ, who brought the Law over to the Church according to the spiritual understanding, leaving the Synagogue derelict.[23]

We must inquire how events, actions and images have been treated in this traditional figuration. We wonder what has become of the image of Bath-Sheba's physical beauty which seduced David, what has happened to the fact that David "lay with her" and made her pregnant before he had any dealing with Uriah, and what has become of Uriah's absolute devotion to the Ark of Israel and to David's army and commander (11.2). We wonder how Christ's Incarnation, Life, crucifixion and victory over Satan are evoked by David's acts—his adultery, his malevolent letter, delivered to Joab by the obedient Uriah. The answer to these inquiries is that the particular actions and images have been virtually negated in the figural understanding. History is dissolved. This seems clear enough, however much we stress that the exegetes believed in the truth of the events. It is the effects of allegory (or "typology") that we are studying, and these I have outlined.

The rationale of such allegory is standard, and Gregory the Great explains it: "often something which is virtuous in the literal sense of the narrative [per historiam], is criminal in the allegorical significance: just as sometimes what is criminal in deed, is virtuous in the book of a prophet." De Lubac demonstrates that this reflects a common idea of the Middle Ages, and it is interesting to note that the principle was

---

[23] For de Lubac, *Exégèse* I.1.401, 457–65; Denis the Carthusian, II.150 C–E: although he decides these are only similes, the tradition is less cautious, as de Lubac shows.

also common in hellenistic allegorical theory.[24] In practice, the exegete actually assumes that "everywhere David signifies Christ."[25]
If this is so, then we have pre-ordained the story's significance, and its
particular images and actions become redundant. David's significance
does not have to be created, or discovered, in a particular context, it
does not have to be concretely present.

Because Donahue and others have claimed that Augustine's great
influence on medieval figural practice shaped it into the "Hebraic"
and "typological" mould, we should look at an example of his own
practice. He deals with the story of Jacob deceiving his father at least
twice, and this will serve to illustrate his figurative procedure.[26] In
Genesis 27 Jacob lies to the old blind Isaac, lies about God, disguises
himself to deceive his blind father and thus manages to steal the elder
brother's blessing. Jacob is presented as the oriental "type" of a
crafty, materially successful man, and as Genesis 27.36 explicitly
states, his name is aptly given, for it means "supplanter". But
Augustine maintains that in this chapter of Genesis there is "no lie,
but a mystery". Really it is an example of those parts of the Bible:

> [which] must be judged to be no lies, but prophetical speeches and
> actions, to be referred to the understanding of those things which
> are true; which are covered as it were with a garb of figure on
> purpose to exercise the sense of the pious enquirer, and that they
> may not become cheap by lying bare and on the surface. . . . [The
> events] are accounted lies only because people do not under-
> stand that the true things which are signified are the things said,
> but believe that false things are the things said.

Perhaps readers are tempted to think that Jacob covers his hands and
neck with the skins of goats' kids to deceive his father into thinking
he, Jacob, is Esau (Genesis 27.11–16), and perhaps readers then
think that Jacob is a crafty, unpleasant liar: "but if this deed be
referred to that for the signifying of which it was really done, by
skins of the kids are signified sins; by him who covered himself
therewith, He who bare not His own but others' sins. The truthful
signification can in no sense be called a lie." As for Genesis 27.16–19,
where Jacob tells his father "I am Esau thy first born", Augustine
comments: "This, if it be referred to those two sins, will seem a lie;
but if to that for the signifying of which those deeds and words were
written, He [Christ] is here to be understood in His body, which is

---

[24] *Exégèse*, I.2.461 (P. Lat. 75.634); J. Pépin, *Mythe et Allégorie* (Paris, 1958),
472; E. Wind, *Pagan Mysteries in the Renaissance* (Peregrine ed., 1967), 27 n. 3,
86 ff.
[25] In *Exégèse*, I.2.463.
[26] *Against Lying*, in *Seventeen Short Treatises of St Augustine* (Oxford, 1874),
426–69; quoting here from 448–50. Jacob, like David was a traditional type of
Christ (see index in P. Lat. 221. 984).

His Church."[27] In a sermon Augustine makes the theological notions involved here even more explicit: Jacob/Christ substitutes himself for guilty Esau/Man and therefore receives the just blessing from father Isaac/father God.[28] The allegory (or, "typology") is technically the Christocentric "allegory of the theologians", but we must ask some questions that are becoming familiar. What has happened to the actions and images so specifically treated in the original? There Jacob's act is depicted as entirely self-advancing, taken on his mother's advice and acted out in relation to a blind, old father whom when he discovers the identity of the man he has been gulled into blessing, "was struck with fear, and astonished exceedingly: and wondering beyond what can be believed . . ." (27.33). Now even if skins of kids could signify "sins" in some context, we wonder what Augustine's *figura* can disclose about the bearer of man's sins in Christian theology, and his "father". Nothing that Augustine would approve, for certain.[29] It is also curious to compare the bearer of man's "sins" that emerges from Augustine's allegorical modes with the Epistle to the Hebrews:

> [Christ] in the days of his flesh, with a strong cry and tears, offering up prayers and supplications to him that was able to save him from death, was heard for his reverence. And whereas indeed he was the Son of God, he learned obedience by the things which he suffered:
>
> (*Hebrews* 5.7–8)

This is similar to Gospel accounts (Matthew 26; Luke 22), and it is hard to see what relation such a Christ has to the smooth worker of Genesis 27 and Augustine's allegory. It cannot even be claimed that Augustine is writing an ironic criticism of orthodox atonement theology. Far from it, he would like us to dissolve the narrative's actions and images into thin air, and he has no subversive intentions.[30]

So far we have seen some examples of later medieval *figura* from Nicholas of Lyra and Denis the Carthusian, but because there has been a rumour among some literary critics that as the Middle Ages grew older allegorical exegesis became extinct, we must now concentrate on this period.[31] In this area de Lubac's work is extremely

---

[27] *Against Lying*, ibid.

[28] See Pontet, *L'Exégèse de St. Augustin*, 164 (Sermon IV. 15 ff.).

[29] For contrast, see G. L. Prestige, *God in Patristic Thought* (London, 1959), 235 ff.

[30] This is a representative enough example, like *Quaest. in Heptateuchum* (CCSL, 1958), I.93; *City of God*, XVIII.44 (number symbolism in Jonah 3.4); *Homily on St John*, 49.2 (allegory of Jairus's daughter, widow's son and Lazarus).

[31] A rumour propagated by Robertson's opponents (see chapter one) and already combatted in his *Preface*, 304–17.

important, but it is perhaps appropriate to note Beryl Smalley's contribution here, since her attempt to plot a twelfth century revolution in exegesis encouraged the rumour I have just mentioned. In an essay in 1963, she pointed out that "the spiritual interpretation continued to flourish" in the fourteenth century, while there was an "extension of the spiritual interpretation from the Bible to profane texts of recent invention". If there had been a movement to emphasize the literal level at some stage, then "the exegetes of the later Middle Ages turned away from it", preferring traditional allegory.[32] After attacking some of Miss Smalley's comments on allegory, Robertson used Holcot without noticing that she herself had published a long essay on this friar, his "pictures" and his allegory, later working this material into a useful book. She stressed that Holcot had little enthusiasm for literal exposition and "concerned himself little with the relation between the author's primary meaning and the spiritual senses".[33] In an article devoted to fourteenth century exegesis she noted the popularity of moralizing allegory (*moralitates*) in the fourteenth century. These show little concern with contexts or literal relations, but were accepted as "more valuable" than the literal gloss and circulated separately. Furthermore, "the old saying that the literal sense is superficial or fleshly and that the spiritual sense is the better object of study" continued to flourish. The fourteenth century had nothing but its greater love of *moralitates* to distinguish it from earlier exegesis.[34] So Beryl Smalley discovers no increase of literalism in the later Middle Ages, quite the contrary. It is strange that Robertson did not notice this more recent work of Miss Smalley, though less strange that his opponents failed to do so.

H. de Lubac confirms Beryl Smalley's work here, finding the later Middle Ages making more and more use of "Philonic" allegory, while the four senses of Christian exegetical theory become split off from any theological dynamic, degenerating into mere formulae and depriving the theory of life.[35] This formulaic use of the four senses was wider than ever ("Partout on le cite, on le commente"), but in de Lubac's view this is simply one of the manifestations of "a deplorable stagnation".[36] Practical application of traditional theory

---

[32] "The Bible in the Middle Ages" in *The Church's Use of the Bible, Past and Present*, ed. D. Nineham, 57–71, see 68, 69, 71; see too J. B. Allen, *The Friar as Critic*, 4–6, 24–5, 42–9 etc.

[33] "Robert Holcot", AFP, 26 (1956), 5–97 (*cf. Preface*, 305 ff.), quotation from 32–3; her book *English Friars and Antiquity* (Oxford, 1960), chapter VII.

[34] *Miscellanea Medievalia*, I (1962), 269, 272–4.

[35] *Exégèse*, II.2.213–14; II.2.300, 308, 310, 315–6: I am not as convinced as Lubac that this is simply a fourteenth-century degeneration, but since my main focus is on the dominant norms in Langland's period there is no need to argue this.

[36] *Exégèse*, II.2.371.

is completely mechanical ("toute mécanique"), while later exegetes are devoted to excessive allegory and the pulverization of texts ("l'excès d'allégorie et la pulvérization du texte").[37] Another characteristic of this epoch is relevant to the present study: the continued popularity of the *Glossa* and the growing number of compilations in prose and verse which were above all else dictionaries of allegories. These helped to freeze traditional symbolism still further.[38] De Lubac also complains that the merging of Christian allegory with nature-symbolism and "the allegory of the poets" became far more pronounced in the later Middle Ages. We have already discussed the confusion of a symbolism which purports to be based on a progressive revelation embodied in historical process with a symbolism based on the timeless cycles of nature and neoplatonic metaphysics, and de Lubac argues that by the fourteenth century this had become a major threat to the existence of an especially Christian allegory, in theory as well as practice.[39] All these factors, de Lubac shows, are combined with "a mixture of allegorizing and ultra-literalism".[40] Such is the position in the age of *Piers Plowman* according to the detailed investigation of de Lubac and Beryl Smalley, and we shall now examine some more exegesis from this period, bearing in mind their claims. They are well grounded.

In de Lubac's opinion Denis the Carthusian is one of the least "decadent" of later medieval exegetes, and it is fair to take him again as a competent representative of Christian *figura* in this period.[41] Denis begins his commentary on Genesis 2 by referring the reader to St Augustine who had insisted that Genesis should be read both literally and spiritually. Denis approves of those "who understand paradise both physically and spiritually", and he was thus handling what was traditionally taken as history, not myth. We will examine his spiritual (allegorical) exposition of this history. At once he glosses the "paradise of pleasure" as "the Church militant". This was a standard interpretation, but if we consider the state and function of the Church militant in the fourteenth and fifteenth centuries, the state described by Langland and the Lollards, then we may begin to suspect this fixed yoking of Paradise and "Church militant" has become an unthinking stereotype.[42] A reader might suspect that the

---

[37] *Exégèse*, II.2.350, 353 and chapter X, *passim*.
[38] *Exégèse*, II.2.372–91; for a vernacular example, "A Middle English treatise on Hermeneutics", ed. R. H. Bowers, *PMLA*, 65 (1950), 590–600.
[39] *Exégèse*, II.2.350, 373–4, 491–3, 505–6, 510; Beryl Smalley, *Study of the Bible*, 243–63.
[40] *Exégèse*, II.2.381–3.
[41] *Exégèse*, II.2.363–7.
[42] Denis the Carthusian, I.2C ff., 27F ff.; for a sense of the condition and role of the Church, see G. Leff, *Heresy in the Later Middle Ages*, 2 vols. (Manchester, 1967); de Lubac, *Exégèse*, II.2.325–510; its role in R. Hilton, *Bond Men Made Free* (London, 1973), 50–3, 227–9.

yoking is intended to serve as an ironic commentary on the contemporary condition, but this has no foundation in Denis's text, for he is simply repeating received terms. In this way any potential challenge in prelapsarian images is ignored. These remarks may gain further point in connection with a criticism Bloomfield made against Huppé and Robertson when reviewing their book on *Piers Plowman*: "the authors assume that Holy Church of Passus I is the church militant. In view of all that Langland has said about the church militant. . . . It is obviously the true and triumphant church which is there personified."[43] Denis too knows something about contemporary conditions in the "church militant", and yet he still produces the old adage, "the paradise of pleasure is the church militant." Were Huppé and Robertson correct in thinking that *Piers Plowman* is "one of the derivatives from the exegetical tradition", criticisms such as Bloomfield's would carry little weight.[44] For the *figura* in exegesis can be completely out of touch with the existential situation of any of its terms, even when the writer has shown elsewhere that he has some consciousness of the situation.

Denis's exegesis of Genesis 3 provides another example. Naturally he understands the tree of Life as Christ. But he also understands the death-dealing tree of Knowledge as Christ. This dual identification was traditional enough. But it is worth seeing *how* from the deadly tree of Knowledge "Christ can be signified"—after all, Christians normally speak of Christ as "the living bread" (John 6.51), "the author of life" (Acts 3.15) and so on. The simplest explanation might be that when reading Genesis 2.9 and its gloss on the tree of Knowledge we should forget the threat and curse of 2.17. Such a fragmenting of the narrative, a "pulvérization du texte" was common enough, as de Lubac shows. But Denis's allegorical procedure is more elaborate than this. The words "knowledge of good and evil" in Genesis 2.9 remind him of Isaiah 7.15, an allegorical prophecy of Christ, where the man to be called Emmanuel will eat butter and honey, "that he may know to refuse the evil, and to choose the good". He takes this text as a gloss on the tree of Genesis 2.9. Here it is useful to remember the popular legend that when the banished Adam was dying, he sent his son Seth back to Eden to seek "oyle of merci". When Seth reached Eden he saw a strange thing: first a fruitless tree with an adder coiling round it; then, looking again, he saw the tree now beautified and reaching up to heaven, while in it sat the Christ-child.[45] The legend offers a striking figuration, and it

---

[43] *Spec*, 27 (1952), 247.
[44] On some consciousness of contemporary situation in Denis's work, *Exégèse*, II.2.364–6; Robertson and Huppé's case is considered below in chapter five.
[45] The legend printed in EETS, 46 (1871), 23 ff.; for the exegetical tradition, B. Smith, *Traditional Images of Charity in Piers Plowman* (The Hague, 1966), 63–4.

illuminates the claim that "as in Adam all die, so also in Christ all shall be made alive" (1 Corinthians 15.22). This, in fact, is the idea that lies behind Denis's gloss on Genesis 2.9. Christ will quell,

> The adversary serpent, and bring back
> Through the world's wilderness long wandered man
> Safe to eternal paradise of rest.
>
> PL XII.312-4

God's acts in history will transform the first great "sin", enacted around the tree of Knowledge, into a *felix culpa*, and so, in a way, the tree of Knowledge will become the tree of Life.

But Denis has short-circuited the dynamics of the idea. He shows no concern for the historical dimension so essential to it, and dissolves any historical vision in his allegory. Nor does he have much concern for the image in its own contexts. He does care for the theological proposition (which he could probably have expressed better without glossing Genesis 2.9) and the figurative image simply becomes an appendage, a rather inconvenient one. There is no attempt to show *how* Christ came to be seen ("designari") in the deadly tree of Knowledge. The theological proposition is a *donnée* whose application here involves both "pulverization" of the text and an evasion of the time-dimensions so basic to any justification of his (orthodox) reading.

In the same chapter of Genesis God takes Adam and puts him "into the paradise of pleasure, to dress it, and to keep it". On the phrase "And the Lord God took man" (2.15), Denis comments, "that is, he led Christ, in his assumed (human) nature, from the most spotless womb of the virgin", while "paradise" is still read as "church".[46] This figuration seems an example of what de Lubac calls a "wholly mechanical" method. The theological complex behind the reading is the famous relationship of the first and second Adam. But it is not at all clear how a reader's understanding of either term of the figuration could be increased by this kind of yoking. Good has just led Adam from outside the garden, where he was created, into the garden itself (2.7–8). In his allegory Denis substitutes Christ for Adam, or rather the incarnate Christ. He must then have asked himself, from where did God lead Christ, and into what; the answer he gives is probably as good as any other we could conjure up having committed ourselves to this method. It is a method which dismisses historical and imagistic context, as well as any nuances of the literary communication.

After Adam and Eve have eaten the forbidden fruit, God enters the garden to punish them: "And when they heard the voice of the Lord

---

[46] Denis the Carthusian, I.27F.

God walking in paradise at the afternoon air, Adam and his wife hid themselves from the face of the Lord God, amidst the trees of paradise" (Genesis 3.8). Denis picks up the phrase "in paradise":

> In paradise: that is in the church militant, to walk abroad in the hearts of his own elect and holy ones . . . because he dwells in them through faith and charity; and they themselves carry him in their hearts only in so far as it is afternoon, that is, after that most burning fire of the holy Spirit which was in the primitive Church. . . .[47]

The situation, Adam and Eve are all dissolved. (In contrast look at *Paradise Lost* X.92–115.) As usual Denis has a set of propositions which he wishes to assert, not explore: he gets his chance because the image puts God in the garden, and this is enough for the exegete to extract his proposition, regardless of contexts. It is hardly surprising that faith, charity and the inspiration of the Holy Spirit are claimed for the "elect", or that these were present in the early Church. But we also know that Adam and Eve were the first of the "elect", and the text of Genesis focuses on their condition at that particular juncture: in the exegete's allegory their condition, the particular juncture and narrative context disappear, while Denis asserts extraneous theological and psychological propositions which are hardly clarified by being involved in this allegory.

Besides Denis the Carthusian we should look at some representative examples of Nicholas of Lyra's allegorical modes, and we can take the story of Abram. In Genesis 11 Abram takes Sarai to be his wife, and Nicholas of Lyra comments, "that is wisdom acquired before". He reads the plain in Genesis 12.6 as "humility" and when, two verses later, the hero reached a mountain on the east of Bethel Lyra notes, "that is, tending to the perfection of religion". That Abram pitched his tent shows him "persevering in good", and when he has to go into Egypt because of famine the allegorist seems to find a justification for his own profession, for Abram was giving "spiritual" food in return for physical food (contrast Genesis 12.10–11). Abram then tells Sarai to say that she is his sister, because he fears that when the Egyptians see how beautiful she is, "they will say: She is his wife. And they will kill me, and keep thee" (12.11–12). To Lyra this means that "the religious ought to call the wisdom which God has given to him his sister."[48] The relation of this to Abram's explicit motives shows that the figuration involves the same prin-

---

[47] I.33F ff.; see too Robertson, "The Doctrine of Charity in Medieval Literary Gardens", *Spec*, 26 (1951), 25–6.
[48] Nicholas of Lyra, I.60D ff.

ciples we discovered earlier in the standard allegory of David's adultery, and the similarity of figurative practice is plain.

We could certainly go on examining examples of figurative practice in late medieval exegesis but by now this should not be necessary.[49] Analysis of exegetical practice has shown the tendency of medieval figuralists to dissolve events and actions, and with these both the text's images and existential dimensions. The handling of images was indeed "wholly mechanical", and Robertson's phrases, "allegorical machinery", "the conventional machinery of spiritual exegesis", seems all too appropriate. As de Lubac said, the effects of such procedure, from almost any viewpoint, is "a deplorable stagnation".[50] Both areas of discourse are frozen into unexamined correlation. This preserves reader or exegete from exploring literary, historical or theological *processes*, from exploring the ways in which propositions have become accepted. Any possible significance in the particular yoking of image and idea is irretrievably lost, and we are left with a dead conservatism. Such then is the dominant figurative mode in the practice of exegesis and we are now prepared to look for the kinds of effect it may have on homiletic and literary allegory.

---

[49] For other representative examples, Nicholas of Lyra, II.63H; I.38D; I.58H; Denis the Carthusian, I.64B ff.
[50] *Preface*, 70; *Exégèse*, II.2.371-2.

3 Preachers and Poets

Pistol: Bardolph, a soldier firm and sound of heart,
And of buxom valour, hath, by cruel fate
And giddy Fortune's furious fickle wheel,
That goddess blind,
That stands upon the rolling restless stone.
Fluellen: By your patience, Aunchient Pistol. Fortune is painted
plind, with a muffler afore her eyes, to signify to you that
Fortune is plind: and she is painted also with a wheel,
to signify to you which is the moral of it, that she is
turning, and inconstant, and mutability, and variation:
and her foot, look you, is fixed upon a spherical stone,
which rolls, and rolls, and rolls: in good truth, the
poet makes a most excellent description of it: Fortune is
an excellent moral.
Pistol: Fortune is Bardolph's foe, and frowns on him;
For he hath stol'n a pax, and hanged must a' be,
A damned death!
Let gallows gape for dog, let man go free
And let not hemp his wind-pipe suffocate.

Shakespeare, Henry V III.6.26–45

We begin with three English sermons (written between 1389 and 1404) which exemplify the characteristics of homiletic allegory in the period. Genesis 14 tells the story of the strife between four kings and the king of Sodom backed by four other monarchs. Describing the expedition of the four kings the preacher explains, "þe secunde kynge, þat is glotenie", while his friends are Sloth and Lechery, the third king is Envy and the fourth is Covetousness. This is precisely the mode employed by Nicholas of Lyra, Denis the Carthusian and the much earlier *Glossa* when reading the same narrative.[1] The second sermon discusses Luke 17.12–14, where Jesus cures ten lepers who beg him to have mercy. An allegory is discovered: "Be þis leprus men

---

[1] *Three Middle English Sermons*, ed. D. M. Grisdale (Kendal, 1939), 53–4 (hereafter cited as Grisdale).

ich vndirstonde a tis tyme al maner o volk þat liggen her e þis world e þe siknes an te sorw of dedli synne"; and as for the leprosy, "lepur is defloratif of fairnes and ter-bi it be-tokenep excesse in etynge and drynkynge." R. P. C. Hanson described Origen's similar interpretation of Jesus' miracles as "essentially anti-historical interpretation which dissolves particularity". We may be so accustomed to finding physical deformity used as a symbol of moral culpability that Hanson's criticism comes as a surprise. But in my view Hanson is justified, for why these particular lepers in this particular context (historical and literary) should be yoked with the banal sentiment that excessive eating and drinking is unattractive, is not immediately clear. Even if we take the lepers as figures of deadly sin, we will be left wondering how deadly sinners so easily recognize God, take the initiative and ask successfully for mercy: after all, Christians usually claimed that one of the effects of "sin" is to blind perception.[2] But the homilist doesn't want anyone to wonder about anything; he has an ethical proposition together with a "machinery" inherited from exegesis, and this machinery allows him to dissolve the images and events sufficiently to assert the general propositions in conjunction with that narrative.

In another of these sermons, the preacher deals with the calling of Abram in Genesis 12. When exegetes interpreted this they read the country and kin from which Abram is summoned as the carnal life.[3] Our preacher finds instead an allegory which means that the country Abram leaves is high heaven, the country he goes to is wretched earth, and "Be this gode, trewe man Abram, ich vndurstonde at tis time vr blessid Lord Crist Iesu." To reach this from Genesis 12 demands that we ignore the details of Abram's summons and journey. Even if we remember St Paul's statement that "[Christ] emptied himself, taking the form of a servant, being made in the likeness of men" (Philippians 2.7), what the preacher's figuration discloses about Abram or Jesus is not at all clear. He does not try to contrast the motives of Jesus and Abram, but simply dissolves the nuances of Genesis 12 and offers us propositions about redemptive actions. The fact that he takes the country from which Abram was called in virtually an opposite sense to some exegetes should occasion little comment, for it was a common principle that things may be glossed *in bono* or *in malo*.[4] It is more important to notice how the homilist's approach to historical acts and literary images is identical

---

[2] Grisdale, 29–30 ("and" expanded); Hanson, *Allegory and Event*, 280; e.g., Christian norms, Thomas Aquinas, *ST*, I–II.86–9; I.48–56; I–II.93.6; vernacular example, *Speculum Christiani*, EETS (1929), sections 4–5.

[3] See Huppé, *Doctrine and Poetry* (New York, 1959), 197, 215–16; Nicholas of Lyra I.60D ff.: basis in Philo's *De Abrahamo* and *De migratione Abrahami*.

[4] Grisdale, 2; *Preface*, 297–8 and the example of David's adultery and killing in the previous chapter.

with the exegetes'. The text is "pulverized", and its particulars become counters to be aligned with, or replaced by, propositions which are not examined. The *locus* of historical drama disappears and, ironically enough, any genuine relation there might perhaps be between Jesus and Abram necessarily disappears with it.

These homilists also illustrate late medieval reading of non-Biblical images. Virgil's second Eclogue begins,

Formosum pastor Corydon ardebat Alexim,
delicias domini, nec, quid speraret, habebat.
(The shepherd Corydon burned with desire for the beautiful Alexis, his master's darling but he had no idea what to expect)

The preacher comments: "Be þis Coridon is vndurstonde Criste and be þis Alexis mannis soule." Having stated this, he finds an allegory of Christ's passion in Virgil's poem and his method, like the exegetes', is "wholly mechanical". He starts off with Coridon, that is Christ; next he must allot various statements to the parts of the poem which seem least uncongenial to these. Similarly, in the second sermon of this collection, the preacher relates how Julius Caesar was murdered, and how the emperor Octavian avenged his death and enforced peace. He then says, "Be þis Octouian ich vndirstonde a tis tyme owr Kyng and owr Emperour Crist." As for Julius Caesar, he is "vr virst vadir Adam" who was "slawyn gostliche" through the Devil's plot. Christ defeated the Devil on the Cross and, in the preacher's strange opinion, left mankind in love and peace.[5] Leaving aside the inaccuracy of the last assertion, we notice that the writer's method destroys contexts and specificity of events—it cannot even be claimed that he is offering an ironical contrast, a relation of "sub-fulfilment", between the imperialistic Octavian and Jesus, the suffering servant crucified by synagogue and state.

A curious aspect of this allegory is its connection with Huppé and Robertson's *Fruyt and Chaf*. There the authors read Chaucer's Octavian in *The Book of the Duchess* as Christ, because Octavian, they claim, is a pun on the numeral for the age of peace, the eighth. Chaucer's poem concludes with "this kyng" riding "homewardes" to a place which is described before the poet awakes from his dream with the castle bell striking twelve. It has usually been accepted that the "ryche hil" and "long castel" included a complimentary acknowledgement of the poet's patron John of Gaunt, alluding to his earldoms of Richmond and Lancaster. Huppé and Robertson, however, understand the "ryche hil" (Rich-mond) as

---

[5] Grisdale, 48–9.

New Jerusalem and claim that Chaucer is depicting Christ the heavenly King returning to the white city of Jerusalem on the rich hill of Sion which is described in the Apocalypse. Both the reading and its method has been forcefully attacked by R. O. Payne, and although Huppé and Robertson's exegesis of Chaucer is of no direct concern here, some of Payne's attack is. He objects that the authors force us to ignore "at least part of the political–historical–geographical identity of Lancaster and Richmond", and he argues that their method "destroys the concrete significance of the text". Furthermore, "the only way to understand the poetry is to know before reading it what it means and then ignore all its parts which would embarrass that meaning, and simply supply from *a priori* assumption any missing but necessary parts".[6] Certainly Huppé and Robertson were led to their allegory by an initial pairing of Christ and Octavian, the very figuration with which we have just seen the preacher begin *his* exposition, and he didn't even feel bound to justify it by the pun Huppé and Robertson use. It is apparent that they have modelled their own practice on the exegetical procedures I have been characterizing. Payne's criticism may hint at this, but his purpose is to combat particular interpretations rather than to pursue the implications which now occupy us. These implications, however, about writing and thinking with allegorical imagery, actually give Huppé and Robertson's methods some interest, for they have turned Chaucer into the kind of religious poet we might expect to emerge from the figurative practices of the later Middle Ages which we have been examining. Perhaps we will come to accept that Huppé and Robertson are more accurate guides to the *norms* of later medieval figural thinking than Auerbach or Donahue. (To suggest this does not of course mean that Chaucer too shared the assumptions and practices common to exegetes, homilists, Robertson and Huppé.)

These norms are again illustrated in the third sermon from the same collection where the writer narrates the well known story of the siege of Athens by the Dorensians. Codrus, the king of Athens, is told by an oracle that Athens will only be saved if he himself is killed by the Dorensians. But the Dorensians' own gods warn them of this, and they are therefore prepared to avoid killing the king of Athens. Codrus then disguises himself in lowly dress and so manages to get himself killed, whereupon the Dorensians, discovering what they have done, go home, and Athens is saved. The homilist discusses the figurative sense: "Be þis peple o Dorens i vndirstonde noþying ell at tis tyme buttle devel and his ostes . . . te peple of Atene, þat is to seie, al mankynde . . . Codrus, þat is vr blessid sauiur, Crist Iesu."

---

[6] *Fruyt and Chaf* (Princeton, 1963), chapter I; *The Works of Chaucer*, ed. F. N. Robinson (2nd edn, 1968), 778 note to ll.1318 ff.; Payne's review in *CL*, 15 (1963), 272–6.

Codrus disguising himself "is" the Incarnation where Jesus "cloþed Him e þe symple wede o mankynde". The preacher is obviously trying to make a model which will disclose the self-humiliation of God in the Incarnation, the devotion of Jesus to men and the Anselmian idea that it was *only* through the Incarnation that man could be saved. But it is once more noticeable that the preacher envisages the relation between model and the claims which he wishes to disclose as that between appendage and self-evident proposition. In this assumption he provides another example of a characteristic de Lubac criticized in fourteenth and fifteenth-century exegesis and allegory: "All is codified, stereotyped."[7] One of the most stark facts about the Crucifixion is the rejection of Jesus: "He came unto his own: and his own received him not" (John 1.11). But in the sermon's figure it is only the devils (Dorensians) who oppose him, and only they who fail to perceive God incarnate (disguised). Images are envisaged as "codified" doctrinal propositions. But if "al mankynde" is already with Christ it is hard to see any point in the suicidal disguise and we are certainly left wondering why the devils disperse. The answer to such queries is that the preacher tries to forestall them by dissolving the images in face of the theological message: we have seen exegetes trying to do this and our assessment of that procedure applies here.

Normal practices in late medieval *figura* can be further illustrated by looking at some constructions around Luke 10.38: "Now it came to pass, as they went, that he [Christ] entered into a certain town [intravit in quoddam castellum]: and a certain woman named Martha received him into her house." By the ninth century, when Raban Maur compiled his allegorical dictionary, it had become an exegetical commonplace that "castellum" signified the Virgin Mary, and that Luke was talking figuratively about the entry of Christ into her womb.[8] This was so standard an interpretation that Luke 10.38–42 became one of the readings in the Mass of the Assumption. The allegorical procedure demands that we ignore the particularity of Luke's images, and it is extremely doubtful whether this makes the doctrine about the conception of Christ any more intelligible. Even the casual tone of the verse's opening is hard to relate to the *figura*, let alone the role of the woman Martha who actually receives Jesus. The exegetes want us to ignore the event and the words in which the event is recorded; at the same time they offer a doctrinal proposition and naively ask us to read it as if it was a statement of the same order as the following note made by Coleridge: "Left Grasmere, Saturday noon, Jan. 14, 1804— on foot / arrived at Kendal after a

---

[7] Grisdale, 67–8; *Exégèse*, II.2.375.
[8] See R. D. Cornelius, *The Figurative Castle* (Bryn Mawr, 1930), 37 ff.; the allegory of course uses an inadequate translation of "castellum".

sweltering walk."[9] To treat a theological proposition in this way does not only necessitate the destruction of images and events: it also involves a pre-critical mishandling of the second area of discourse in which the preacher or exegete is especially interested, the theological. It is pre-critical because there is no conscious intention to challenge a traditional "mystery" or "disclosure model": we are meeting incompetence rather than subversiveness.

The homilist Mirk delivers a vernacular sermon for the Virgin's Assumption, in which he comments on Luke's text:

> Scho was þe castell þat Ihesu entred into; for ryght as a castell hath dyuerse propyrtes þat longyth to a castell þat schall be byge and strong, ryght so had our lady dyuerse vertues þat made hur abolle befor all woymen forto receyue Christ.[10]

Mirk's debts to the exegetes' reading habits are patent and there is no need to repeat the commentary I have just offered. But the mode in which Mirk expands his figuration is interesting because it again shows us writing which develops from exegetical allegory. He elaborates his own images in describing the castle and its structure, and he then reveals how he understands allegorical images. The castle's ditch is a ditch of "mekeness" and the water in the moat "ys compassyon"; the Virgin,

> wepte blode ouer this dyche lyke a drawbrygge þat schall be drawen up aȝenys enmys and lete downe to frendys þat wyl kepe þys castel. . . . By þys bryge ȝe schull undyrstond discret obedyens. . . .

> Thys castell ys dowbull-wald: a forther þat ys lowyr, and a hyndyr þat ys heghyr. Tha forthyr bytokenyth wedloke; . . . . Alsoo þe forther wall bytokenyth pacience, þe hyndyr bytokeneth virginite . . . maydenhode.[11]

It is totally obscure how the contents of such disparate notions as virginity, compassion, marriage and the virgin-mother of God are to be disclosed by this imagistic procedure. Nevertheless, the passage represents that combination of "allegory and ultra-literalism" which de Lubac found characteristic of late medieval exegesis and symbolism, that procedure where "all is codified".[12]

Other passages in Mirk show how his methods are similar to those of exegetes. In his twenty-third sermon he gives an interpretation of

---

[9] *The Notebooks*, ed. K. Coburn (New York, 1957 ff.), entry 1843.
[10] Mirk's Festial, EETS, 96 (1905), 228.
[11] *Festial*, 229–30.
[12] See *Exégèse*, II.2.381, 375.

the five loaves and two fishes with which Christ fed five thousand people (Mark 6.39–46):

The fyrst lofe of þes V ys contycyon of hert. The second ys trew schyrft of mouþe. The þryd ys satysfaccyon. The IIII ys drede of redemacion, þat ys of turnyng aʒeynne from hys synne; . . . . The V ys persauvaracyon in God. The two fyschys ben oryson and almes dedes, for thes ben noresched yn terus of deuocyon.[13]

Particular times and images, total contexts, these are unimportant flotsam. The approach is akin to ones already discussed, but it is worth seeing a fourteenth-century exegete exploring the figurative potential of the continuation of the same text:

The ship is the human body in which, according to the platonists, the soul resides just as a sailor in a ship: in which it is driven and sometimes endangered by the waves of passions of wrath and concupiscence (which are in the physical organs). For the movement of passion sometimes overturns reason.

When he comments on the parallel text in Matthew 14.24, Nicholas of Lyra again finds a figure, but this time he says of the ship tossed in the sea, "that is the church disturbed by persecutions."[14] In both cases his approach to possible figurative resonance is the same, and it is an approach shared by preachers.

Jean Gerson's sermons are typical of the period (early fifteenth century) in being replete with such figural methods. Discussing the nativity he explains the significance of the shepherds' vision:

Par quoy nous est monstrée que ung seigneur se il veille diligemment a garder son pays. . . . Dieu se monstrera a luy et aussy a chascune personne qui veille a garder sa seule brebis qui luy est commise, c'est son ame.

It is this vision which David figures ("figure") when he writes, "I have gone astray like a sheep that is lost" (Psalm 118.176). This approach encourages Gerson to write an elaborate figural sermon around Jesus' words in John 14.23: "If any one love me, he will keep my word. And my Father will love him: and we will come to him and make our abode with him." Gerson isolates the word "abode [mansionem]" and tells how souls must be hosts to God: "Garde que ton hostel soit nectoiez et despeschiez de tout ce qui desplaire." God is the Lord who wishes to visit, "l'ostel de ta conscience". You

---

[13] *Festial*, 104.
[14] Nicholas of Lyra, VI.101H–102C (*cf. Piers Plowman* B VIII.29 ff.) and VI.48.

must therefore clear out all the dirt of sin, avarice, ire and so on, and for this you must employ, "III chamberies en l'ostel de ta conscience: *Oroison, Obeissance, Pais et Union*". He goes on to describe, in detail, their tasks in preparing the house for the Holy Spirit. For example, when you have fears of death and hell this is the Holy Spirit thundering at the door and you should send *Obeissance* to open the door, which is to say, "que tu dois corrigier, tu dois amender ta vie selond les commendements de Dieu". As for the Holy Spirit, he'll smash in the windows and if the door isn't opened you'll go to hell. The mode is familiar enough and further illustrated by the meals in the house: "la table de sobresse, la chandelle de vray(e) foy, le pain de sapience, le vain de compunction, le sel de discrecion, le fruit de bonnes oeuvres."[15] Again, all is "codified" and the customary mixture of allegory and literalism appears in the figurative writing. But the literalism is unconstructive since we are still meant to read the images in a way which makes them redundant, taking them as transparent and accepting the writers assumption that his discursive statements and his imperatives make adequate sense on their own.

If we look at *Le Livre de Seyntz Medicines*, written by an English aristocrat virtually contemporary with Langland, we find the standard kind of figurative procedures displayed. At one point the author, Henry of Lancaster, describes how foxes act maliciously then return to their holes where they multiply. Once in their holes they are easily caught, either by terriers or by sticking a rod into the hole to force the fox out. Alternatively, their holes are blocked while they are away and they are then easily chased and caught by dogs, because they stink. These foxes, Henry writes, "sont les sept mortels pecchés", while their lair is Henry's heart. The little dog sent into the hole, "est ma conscience", the hunter who thrusts the rod into the hole, "c'est mon confesseur" and the rod itself, "est les bones doctrines et les bones enseignements . . . et meynt bon ensample". The rod is composed of three smaller rods which are Confession, Contrition and firm hope of Mercy. It is normal enough to externalize psychological and moral relations.[16] But once more we find that despite Henry's relish of hunting, the images and actions are so transparent that the reason for their presence is hardly clear. For the narrative, naturally enough, does not show the hole reacting to the dog or to the hunter's four part rod; furthermore, the dog is the hunter's, not the hole's. If we push through this commentary the *exemplum* falls apart. At once it will be objected that such commentary is crudely literalistic and mechanical; it is like those old-

---

[15] Jean Gerson, *Six vermons Français Inedits*, ed. L. Mourin (Paris, 1946), 71–84, 296–7.
[16] *Le Livre de Seyntz Medicines*, ed. E. J. Arnold (Oxford, 1940), 103–16; on externalizing, see *Preface*, 34–5.

fashioned critics who thought allegory necessitated a 1:1 correlation between terms. Now this is undeniable, but it is also legitimate and inevitable when the writing itself manifests the kind of "mixture of allegory and ultra-literalism" we have described. The mixture encourages a kind of allegory which led E. H. Gombrich to write of, "the ping pong of it all".[17]

Such is the dominant figurative mode developed by preachers and further illustration would be superfluous. I would, however, like to conclude this section by taking two brief examples from a fifteenth-century translation of the extremely popular *Speculum humanae salvationis*.[18] Chapter thirteen states that Christ's temptations were gluttony, pride and avarice. His victory over the last temptation had been prefigured:

> This ffigurid David sleyng a bere and a lyonne ffor thas two beestis betakened auarice

This refers to 1 Kings (Samuel) 17.34–7, where David told Saul that he was ready to fight Goliath—God had delivered him out of the paw of the bear and the lion and would deliver him from Goliath. The figural relationship the writer sets up between Christ's temptations and David's victories depends on a figural understanding of the Old Testament bear and lion, turning them into signs of avarice. This typology/allegory is anti-historic and destroys literary and historical contexts; in doing so, as one finds time and again, the ironical result is that the historical and theological role of Jesus in relation to the Old Testament, which typology is designed to illuminate, is not disclosed at all. Jesus and the figurative foreshadow are flattened into the neat scheme of victory over "deadly sins" and the temporal dynamic between the two Testaments is of no interest. Similar effects result from his handling of the Samson–Christ typology which he invokes when depicting how Jesus was mocked:

> Nowe Sampson it is to witt for his grettest stroungnesse,
> Prefigured oure lord Crist
>
> (*Chapter XIX*)

In case we are not impressed by the ground of the *figura*, the poet recalls how Samson "vengid hym" against his mockers, the Philistines, who are "prefiguryng" the Jews, and warns his readers that

---

[17] In *Art and Illusion* (3rd edn, 1968), 315.
[18] It would be a pity not to mention the representative *Gesta Romanorum* EETS, 33 (1879), e.g., 148 ff. The edition of the Speculum used here is *The Miroure of Mannes Saluacion* (London, 1888): on its popularity, P. Perdrizet, *Etude sur le Speculum Humanae Salvationis* (Paris, 1908), 4–5.

Christ too will avenge himself against all sinners at the Last Judgement. The relationship between Christ and Samson becomes utterly wooden as the figuralist levels out historical process and historical difference. Samson's sub-fulfillment of Jesus' task, the great limitations of his vision, imperialistic and militaristic, these are as vital to any meaningful connections between Samson and Christ as is the Nazarite's supernatural gift of physical strength. The relations between Samson's suicidal vengeance and the Christian doctrine of Christ's role at the "Last Judgement" is also extraordinarily obscure. Perhaps the root of such problems is the way both historical dynamic and any attention to existential situations had been jettisoned from figurative writing and reading.

We shall now look at two extremely popular late medieval poets who often write figuratively "with mysty colour of cloudes derke / . . . Clokynge a trouthe with colour tenebrous". According to Rosemond Tuve, Deguileville illustrates the admirable virtues of allegorical imagery. She believes that these admirable qualities are explained by the tradition of figurative exegesis: "centuries of familiarity with religious allegory strictly so-called—mainly typological, scripture read mystice, history seen as God's dimly apprehended revelation of 'truth'."[19] A later medieval allegory which is closely related to exegetical practice and so to the concomitant practice of preachers (both already analysed), and which also has the historical dimension and other traits Miss Tuve admires, would indeed be a most rare and astonishing poem. We should, in fact, be very sceptical about claims which maintain that a poem with the qualities Miss Tuve describes is closely related to the practice of exegetes and homilists reading and writing "mystice", or allegorically. We can test out such claims by examining some of the characteristic uses of *figura* in Deguileville's *Pèlerinage de la Vie Humaine*.[20]

It is appropriate to begin with an example of what Miss Tuve so well describes as his "habit of literalizing figures of speech". She associates this with typological habits and explains that "this technique related to the basic functioning of allegory as a mode that could make notions and ideas interact narratively by imaging them in their symbolic forms." This may be a possible definition of "the basic functioning of allegory". But it conceals problems instead of

---

[19] The quotation preceding Tuve is from Hawes, *Pastime of Pleasure*, EETS, 173 (1927), 11. 705 ff; Tuve, *Allegorical Imagery*, chapter III, especially 160–1, 164–5, 169, 172, 183–4, 198–9.

[20] I use Lydgate's translation of the second redaction of the *Pèlerinage de la vie humaine*, in EETS, 77, 83, 92 (1899–1904) rather than Stürzinger's edition of the first French version of 1331 (Roxburghe Club, London, 1893): because it is more easily accessible, and because the limitations of Lydgate's allegorical writing do not misrepresent the original—this is corroborated by the comments on Deguileville's *Pèlerinage de l'âme* which follow.

solving them. Does Miss Tuve's sentence imply that ideas each have "their" own proper symbolical form (that is, are ideas in allegory always represented as in emblem books or bestiaries)? How are we to find out whether the image is actually "imaging" the ideas, or whether it is simply acting as a sign—like a signpost saying "York" in relation to the city of York, or even like the formula MC_2 in relation to energy? What do we mean by "imaging"? These questions can only be faced satisfactorily by examining particular works, and this is precisely the knowledge we can extract from Miss Tuve's assertion. "Function", "imaging" and "interact", are all words which suggest a process whose presence could be pointed out within a structure; or, alternatively, one whose absence might be demonstrated. Because of these possibilities we must not be persuaded against analysing particular pieces of allegorical writing by Miss Tuve's generous *a priori* definitions, nor must we be intimidated by her scorn of post-renaissance thinking about symbolism.[21]

Miss Tuve spends two paragraphs on Deguileville's image of Dame Penance. She finds that it provides a classic example of "a pleasure native to allegorical reading", and the naming of the figure "is only the beginning of our understanding of what she means; indeed, this is perhaps to be evoked largely from our own experience of contrition." Miss Tuve then connects "allegorical reading" with literature which evokes reflection on experience. It is obviously fair to take this passage as representative of the poet's allegorical modes.[22]

Deguileville's lady appears holding "an hamer" in one hand, "a yerde" in the other and "a bysme in hyr mouth / Atwyxe hyr teth" (4014–5). Miss Tuve attacked nineteenth-century "misconceptions of allegory" which falsely supposed that the allegorist intended "a realistically credible tale". This seems a just attack; but one wonders, in that case, why the poet follows his figure's entry with remarks on her appearance such as these:

> Wher-off I hadde gret mervayl
> . . .
> But yiff a-nother (to my devys,)
> Hadde holde yt so as dyde she,
> Men wolde ha sayde, she haddle be
> Out of hyr wyt, or elly falle
> In-to rage.
>   (4016; 4020–4)

And before she first speaks the poet assures us that "the bysme lette her neueradel / But that she myght speke wel" (4027–8). These

---

[21] *Allegorical Imagery*, 200 (see 198–200), 3, 128 n. 46 etc.
[22] *Pilgrimage*, ll. 3989–4573; *Allegorical Imagery*, 161–2.

comments suggest precisely that "mixture of allegory and ultra-literalism" which we have so often met in this period's *figura*.[23] The poet himself is responding to the emblem as if it were part of a "realistically" conceived tale, and he expects his audience to be doing the same. When Penance notices how she is being stared at she informs the spectators that they have not understood her emblematic properties, what they "synefye" (4035-6). To correct this state of affairs she will "expone feythfully" her significance. She is "callyd Dame Penaunce" and is chief warden,

> Off thylke yle most secre;
> The wych (who so espye kan,)
> Ys yhyd with-Inne a man;
> (4056-8)

Her properties, she continues, are for keeping this island clean. It seems to be from this stage onwards that Miss Tuve thinks Deguile-ville causes a "deliberate reflection on experience", and from here that he "evoked" the full understanding of penitential theory and experience. Certainly Penance states that she is concerned with what "ys yhyd with-Inne a man", and the ensuing description of her activities should be particularly instructive.

The poet depicts how she cleans out "fylthe and al ordure", and the mode is very similar to the one found in works already discussed —like Gerson's sermons or *Le Livre de Seyntz Medicines*. Penance relates how she used her hammer on the heart of Mary Magdalene, and made her weep, so greatly that:

> She was wasshe with-al so clene
> And so inly purefyed,
> That there was no felthe espyed
> Off synne with-Inne hyr tendre herte.
> (4128-31)

And then comes the "ultra-literalism" within the allegory, a feature so typical in late medieval allegory:

> ffor, whan the bytter terys smerte
> Off hyr wepyng wer Ronne down
> Thorgh sorwe and gret contrycioun,
> I took vn- to hem so gret kepe,
> That I hem gadrede on an hepe,
> That ordure leffte noon be-hynde.

---

[23] *Exégèse*, II.2.381; *Allegorical Imagery*, 161 n. 11.

And I to-gydre dyde ham bynde—

. . .

And make ther-off a lye strong, That ther-with-al (I yow ensure,)
I wasshe a-way al ordure.

(4132–8; 4140–2)

Dame Penance is therefore called God's "Lavendere" and his
"chaumberere". She describes in detail how she uses her hammer to
destroy the worm of conscience by also destroying its container,
which is like a "stynkyng and horryble" pot that can only be cleaned
by breaking.[24] She follows this by exhorting her audience to understand that she is conveying doctrine about contrition (4184–6), and
the poet himself again demonstrates how figurative imagery functions
in his kind of writing, as he carefully explicates the relations between
the poet and a man's "synnes":

> But, lyk the pot, he most hem breke,
> And no theng in the asshes reke.
> I mene as thus: conceyveth al,
> Thogh that a pot be broke smal
> On sherdys and on pecys ek,
> Yet al yt ys nat worth a lek,
> But euery sherd be cercyd wel
> Touchynge hys ordure euerydel,
> And yscrapyd clene a-way,
> Ye mot hem breke in gret affray,
> That felthe noon ther-in abyde;
> ffor wych ye moste well provyde
> With sobbyng and with syhes depe
> And salte terys that ye wepe,
> And other peynys sharpe and smerte;
> Thynkynge thus with-Inne your herte;

(4193–208)

Penance then compiles a questionnaire: did you offend on Sunday or
Monday; at what time; what were the "cycrcumstauncys and the
manere"; did you resist; did you encourage temptation, and so on.
This returns her to the relations between "the worm of conscience",
the pot and the hammer.[25] She beats the worm with her hammer and,
being the poet's exegete, explains:

> And thus, yiff ye take hede a-ryght,
> Thys the sygnyfycacioun

---

[24] *Pilgrimage*, ll. 4154–83, 4196–203, 4243–251, 4259 ff., etc.
[25] *Pilgrimage*, ll. 4208 ff.

> And verray exposicioun
> Off thy hamer that ye her se;
> The whych ys namyd, ek off me,
> . . .
> Nat ellys but contrycioun.
>
> (4308–12; 4313–4)

She thus fulfils her promise to tell us "what thyng yt doth sygnefye".
I have quoted at some length to let the poet himself show how he
thinks images "sygnefye". Miss Tuve derided, as another of the
nineteenth-century misconceptions of allegory, the view that
allegory is "translated philosophy, logical discourse or argument
set down in picture-language". I would not want to make any
claims for the "logic" of the writing, but from the fully representative examples we have just looked at it seems that the allegorical
image is indeed being taken as a picture model.[26] Deguileville tells us
that the section on the hammer and the pot is "doctryne . . . touch-
yng verray contrycioun", and he gives a series of similar descriptions,
showing Penance hammering at a filthy pot to clean out filth and
worm. From this picture model, for such it is, he reads off the
correlating "doctryne" about the area of penance. In this way he
moves from hammer and pot to contrition, sobbing, salt tears and
pains "with-Inne your herte". He comments that "the pot ys broke /
on pecys smale up and doun, / By verray trew contricioun" (4292–4).
And when he adds that the hammer is "Nat ellys but contricioun",
he is clearly reading off a doctrinal and psychological complex from
his allegorical model. It is hard to see what other kind of relation or
interaction he sets up between hammer-pot-worm-filth → tears:
and, contrition-iniquity-worm of conscience-filth of sin → tears. If
this reading seems literalistic, then by now it should be obvious that
this quality is part of the allegory itself. A similar assessment is
demanded by Deguileville's handling of his model of the "bysme"
and its relations to confession (4324–552). Here the obscure theological notion of "satysfaccyoun" is read off the model describing
the rod's uses. Both medieval translator and the original poet un-
consciously treat the complex doctrinal language as if equivalent to
his own "scale model". This employment of allegorical images
implies an underestimation, if not a complete unawareness, of the
different nature of the second term. The glib correlations encourage readers to accept talk about "satysfaccyoun" as if it were
simply discourse of the same order as the model, with its chastizing
school-"maystresse" and chastized children; but the acceptance

---

[26] Other similar examples, ll. 4324–561, 23936–87: cf. *Allegorical Imagery*, 161
n. 11.

PREACHERS AND POETS **47**

encouraged is mindless—not one which will invite the reader to
explore the moral and ideological role of the orthodox school
teacher and then to feed his discoveries here into the area of discourse to which the model is pointing. It is, in fact, a naive picture
model, as inadequate for developing a constructive critique of
orthodox theology and ethics as for defending and developing orthodox religious thought and language.[27] This is the mode which
dominated late medieval *figura*.

In his later pilgrimage, *Pèlerinage de l'Ame*, Deguileville wrote an
allegory around the Christian account of man's redemption.[28] The
imagery employs a dry tree and a green tree, as in the Legends of the
Cross mentioned in chapter two. In Guillaume's *Ame* the pilgrim's
soul has been tried, found guilty and only saved by Christ's charter.
He has seen hell in macabre detail, purgatory, and is en route to
paradise. He comes across a lovely, flourishing green tree, and alongside it a dried-up tree (5594-6). Some pilgrims are comforted by an
apple. This is the apple which had been grafted into the dry tree
from the green tree, through the crucifixion (5591 ff.). This grafting
was necessary because Adam had taken an apple from the first tree,
"de toute contre droit" (5870), whereupon it became dried up and
barren, thenceforth reflecting man's fallen state. Man is damned
unless someone restores to the tree, "autel pomme ou melleur asses"
(5874). The angel exegete explains to Guillaume that the comforting
apple could only grow on the tree of Jesse, the green tree, whose
leaves have various allegorical meanings. This green tree also contains the Virgin Mary (5687 ff.). Then at the crucifixion the good
apple was nailed onto the dry tree which is revived by the "precieus
jus" flowing from that apple (6100-658). The tree which had been
dry now also becomes green and provides the saving fruit (6655-98).
This restoration releases man from inevitable damnation.

In an article on the traditions of "The Child in the Tree", E. S.
Greenhill discusses this episode in relation to antecedents, and she
notices that "there are certain anomalies in Guillaume's narrative."
As she says, the tree which at lines 6655 ff. exults in its restoration is
in fact presented to the pilgrim and us as still being withered and
unredeemed—"seche sens humeur" (5596). Another of the
"anomalies" is that the apple comforting the pilgrims is used to
suggest the Eucharistic food, although the tree is shown as still dry:
the angel says at the beginning that the apple is the one which "pour
li / en ce haut arbre sec pendi". Why then is the tree still dry? She
thinks the answer to her question lies in Deguileville's failure to

[27] See my discussion at the end of chapter one, above, with notes 41-2.
[28] *Pèlerinage de l'Ame*, ed. J. Stürzinger (Roxburghe Club, 1895): see ll. 5583-
6702. Line numbers in text refer to this edition. For Legends of the Cross
mentioned in this paragraph, *EETS*, 46 (1871); see also Ezekiel 17.22-4.

harmonize different sources.[29] This may well be part of the cause, but I think there is a yet more fundamental explanation of the "anomalies" she pointed out.

Deguileville also depicts an argument between the green tree, free from stain, and the dry tree. The green tree asserts that there is no reason why its fruit should be given to the dry tree, although the latter pleads it would be "grand medicinement" for its roots and for all mankind. A debate follows between the persons of the Trinity, and concludes with the Son agreeing to descend to the Virgin, or green tree, and there become an apple ("pomme devendras", 6298) to appease "Justice". The green tree at once breaks into a long complaint, a traditional *Planctus Virginis* as well as an exhortation to make good use of the apple.[30] This paraphrase is necessary to make it clear that Deguileville is trying to present a very full survey of Christian theology of the redemption. Now it is essential to this theology that salvation is achieved "only through time".[31] So Deguileville has to *involve* his allegorical imagery with a traditional temporal dimension. This necessity proved beyond the capabilities of his dominant figurative mode—a mode we have examined in this and the previous chapter. Although he has been saved by Christ's charter and the Virgin's pleas at the beginning of the *Pèlerinage*, when he came to write about the acts and theology of the Redemption, he found that to use his habitual picturing models he first of all had to ignore the contexts of his own "pilgrimage". Unlike Langland, as we shall see, Deguileville has no way of integrating the vision of time present and time past. Instead we are offered an inset picture model of the Redemption. We have already discussed his handling of "satysfaccyoun" in his first *Pèlerinage*, and the theology of the total redemptive process is even less amenable to naive picture models. From the dry tree, green tree, nailing on of the apple and revivification of the dry tree, he tries to read off certain stages in the movement from fall to redemption, together with accompanying propositions. And so, when he wishes to contrast the fallen and redeemed states, he shows us the dry tree and the green tree with redeemed souls playing with the vital apple beneath it. Here the anomaly E. S. Greenhill noted does not trouble Deguileville because he assumes he can evade problems of relation and of time: he simply takes from the picture model the information he wishes to give about a particular area of the Redemption. He therefore ignores at this point the question of the interrelation of his allegorical images—the two trees, the com-

---

[29] Eleanor S. Greenhill, "The Child in the Tree: A Study of Cosmological Tree in Christian Tradition", *Traditio*, 10 (1954), 323–71, here see 354–7.

[30] A. Jeanroy, "La Passion de Nostre Dame et *Le Pèlerinage de l'Ame*", *Romania*, 36 (1907), 363–5.

[31] See Augustine, *On the Trinity*, IV.18.24 (IV *passim*).

forting apple, the playing pilgrims. He hopes to make us read off precisely what his exegete does, and to avoid exploring the images or the propositions. In this way he might hope to stifle Greenhill's queries. Instead of facing such questions, he uses his angelic exegete to write us another model; the pilgrim souls disappear as he recounts an apparently pre-Crucifixion stage in the altercation of the two trees. The crucial temporal dynamic of Christian salvation history is still ignored as after the Fall the dry tree itself understands exactly how it can be revivified and pleads for the "grand medicinement" for mankind. This happens before the Son is shown agreeing to "become an apple" (6298). From the altercation, and its images, comes the information that the fruit to benefit the dry root will benefit "le lignage humain". The poet presumably intended to keep apart this picture and its predecessor (the two trees, pilgrims and saving apple) thus avoiding Greenhill's awkward objections. This picture in turn gives way to the *Planctus Virginis* by the green tree, the exhortation to man and the allegorical crucifixion with its restorative effects. In describing the nailing of the apple onto the dry tree and the immediate effect of the juice, the poet again exemplifies the "ultra-literalism" within allegory which we have met so often. Once again the doctrinal propositions are simply subtracted, not explored, while the historical dynamic still seems of no concern to the poet thinking about the orthodox theology of salvation.

We must conclude that Deguileville's picturing models, his chief allegorical mode in fact, can rarely handle the problems his subject involves. His mode seems antithetical to the one Miss Tuve described so enthusiastically. She, we remember, wrote of "a mode that could make notions and ideas *interact* narratively by imaging them". The word I have italicized actually points towards one area of the inadequacies in Deguileville's mode for handling complex "notions and ideas" as well as historical process. The analysis offered in this book should make it apparent that this mode was not peculiar to Deguileville. Quite the contrary, we see that it dominated late medieval figurative writing in all areas. Against this background we will be better prepared to appreciate precisely how Langland faced similar problems: for example we shall find that the historical dimension which Deguileville ignores in his picture models, Langland integrates into a rather different structure of images. But this anticipates chapter five.

Having raised the important issue of the way a poet handles historical dimensions, it is relevant to mention the comments of two recent critics on that most popular late medieval poet, John Lydgate, before briefly considering an example of his *figura*. R. W. Ayers shows that for Lydgate, typical here of the Middle Ages, history is a book of *exempla* which illustrate accepted proverbs: "The oneness of God and the sameness of man from generation unto generation ensure the constancy of the moral relation. . . . The events of time become the pattern of eternity." Ayers' understanding of Lydgate's methods is particularly interesting in relation to the allegorical modes we have been analysing:

> his narrative procedure understandably resembles that of the typical medieval illustrative pulpit narrative—the exemplum. Each episode is immediately and appropriately followed by elucidation in moral terms, with such resulting alternations of narrative and moralizing passages. . . .

We have traced the implications of these procedures in figurative writing. Lydgate, Ayers continues, "viewed human action as the expression of pre-existing—not developing—moral characteristics".[32] It is striking that the approach Ayers outlines is one R. G. Collingwood thought characteristic of the "rigorously anti-historic metaphysics" of the Greeks. For them, Collingwood argues, history had an exemplary value for human life "simply because the rhythm of its changes is likely to repeat itself". While Ayers discusses Lydgate's (typically medieval) assumption that human actions express unchanging moral characteristics, Collingwood believes that Tacitus represents peculiarly hellenistic habits of mind where "the idea of the development in a character, an idea so familiar to ourselves, is to him a metaphysical impossibility." Just so, Ayers writes that to Lydgate "time, place, costume and even persons, are accidents not affecting the essential truth and validity of the moral propositions."[33] Such approaches to events and actions, time and images are, we have found, truly commonplace. The other study which is also relevant here is D. A. Pearsall's *Lydgate*. He demonstrates how central a representative of later medieval orthodoxy and custom John Lydgate is, and shows how in his understanding of history "the ultimate purpose is to deny history in the interests of truth, so that Hector, Achilles, and the rest may take place in the universal diagram." He comments on "the ease with which human misfortune can be accommodated to a set moral scheme", and argues that such an approach fails to present even the moral scheme with coherence or conviction.[34] This failing too, whereby the second area of discourse is

---

[32] "Medieval History, Moral Purpose and the Structure of Lydgate's *Siege of Thebes*", *PMLA*, 73 (1958), 463–74, especially 465–71.

[33] R. G. Collingwood, *The Idea of History* (London, 1966), 20, 23, 44; Ayers, *op cit*, 473. The objection that Lydgate's and medieval bias is only apparently anti-historic, whereas hellenistic bias is really so, would manifest the same failure to distinguish theory and practice criticized in previous chapters, and overlook the fact that my present purpose is to explore literary modes, not to study disembodied doctrine but only in so far as it is realized in literary productions.

[34] *John Lydgate* (London, 1970), 129, 208: see chapters V, VII, VIII.

also handled ineptly, is itself commonplace in the figurative writing and reading of exegetes and preachers.

In the second book of the *Life of our Lady*, Lydgate deals with 3 Kings (Samuel) 10.18–20, normally read as a figure for the Virgin Mary.[35] Solomon made an ivory throne overlaid with best gold; the throne had six steps with twelve lions beside the steps. This description comes in a chapter depicting the great material wealth and success of Solomon immediately before his "strange women" led him to prefer "strange gods" (3 Kings 11). Lydgate ponders the relation between the image and the figured Virgin:

> She was the trone, where that Salamon
> For worthynesse, sette his riall see
> . . .
> The golde was love, the yvory chastyte
> And xii leouns so grete huge and large
>
> Of the old Lawe, werne the propheteȝ twelffe
> That longe aforne gan beholde and see
> That Salamon, goddys sone hymself
> Shulde in þis maide be holde his rial see
> (II.610–11; 617–23)

This manifests the dominant traits of medieval figural writing, as our analysis has shown. The Old Testament image is plucked from its contexts; the Solomon–Christ relationship is frozen into a fixity as far as the figuralist is concerned, and the account of Solomon's development in the very next chapter is negated. The poet treats the Old Testament image as a picturing model from which we can extract the relevant theological information about Mary, her qualities ("the golde was love, the yvorye chastyte"), her relation to her son, "that Salamon, goddys sone hymself", and to those long range forecasters, "xii leouns . . . werne the propheteȝ twelffe". This model is normal enough and reveals the habitual inadequacies I have discussed in some detail. The poet unwarily encourages us to make a simple correlation between two disparate realms of discourse. Thus, we ask *how* Jesus in Mary's womb is so easily correlated to Solomon on his throne, and in pushing on with such questions we may find that the "mystery" of the Incarnation is being dissolved by the writer's allegorical mode—dissolved through incompetence rather than subjected to any powerful critique.

---

[35] *Life of our Lady*, ed. J. Lauritis *et al.* (Pittsburgh, 1961).

4 Shells and Kernels: Models of Allegory

A thousand tymes have I herd men telle
That ther ys joy in hevene and peyne in helle,
And I acorde wel that it ys so;
But, natheles, yet wot I wel also
That there nis noon dwellyng in this contree,
That eyther hath in hevene or helle ybe,
Ne may of hit noon other weyes witen,
But as he hath herd seyd, or founde it writen;
For by assay ther may no man it preve.
But God forbede but men shulde leve
Wel more thing then men han seen with ye!
Men shal not wenen every thing a lye
But yf himself yt seeth, or elles dooth;
For, God wot, thing is never the lasse sooth,
Thogh every wight ne may it nat ysee.
Bernard the monk ne saugh nat all, pardee!
Chaucer, *The Legend of Good Women*, Prologue, F.

Hard to express that sense of the analogy or likeness of a Thing
which enables a Symbol to represent it, so that we think of the
Thing itself—and yet knowing that the Thing is not present to us.
Coleridge, *Notebooks* 2274 (November 1804)

We have studied figural practices at some length and should now
spend a little more time on the critical models which guided thought
about the justification of allegorical expression. St Thomas Aquinas
thought that poets use metaphor simply because men like representing things and metaphor is a way of doing so. In the poet's figurations
"the literal sense is not the figure of speech itself, but the object it
figures." Poetic allegory is a species of parable and its referent, the
object figured ("id quod figuratur") could be expressed in plain,
literal prose without any loss of meaning. Since the sole motive for
metaphor is the "delight" men take in "representation" it is hardly
surprising that Thomas regards poetry and its figurative language as a
form of verbal trickery which is only one grade above the lowest
discourse—sophistic. On these grounds he attacks Plato's methods

of teaching, rather than the contents of his teaching. The trouble with Plato, according to Thomas, is that he continually obscures his literal meaning by using figurative language and "teaching by symbols".[1] He is unambiguous about the status of poetry and its *figura*: "The science of poetry is about things which because of their deficience of truth [propter defectum veritatis] cannot be laid hold of by the reason. Hence the reason has to be drawn off to the side by means of certain comparisons."[2] So although poetry and theology may both seem to use symbolic expression, in poetry that which is figured is either sub-rational or, if it is rational, could have been expressed more lucidly and efficiently in plain literal discourse. Theology and the Bible, on the other hand, employ figurative modes "for their indispensable usefulness" in disclosing truths which "transcend" present capacities of rational cognition and expression. This, he believes, is very different to the poet's reasons for allegory. His argument presents a conventional position clearly and cannot be ignored.[3]

In thinking about figurative expression here it is instructive to turn to the influential Augustine. In a fairly well known passage he discusses the subject in relation to Canticle 4.2: "Thy teeth as flocks of sheep, that are shorn, which come up from the washing, all with twins: and there is none barren among them." The text comes in a section where the lover is evoking the beloved's beauty by a series of rich similes. Augustine understands the verse normally enough when he envisages the teeth as saints of the Church cutting men off from their errors, softening their hardness (biting and chewing) and then transferring them to the Church's body. He also "recognizes" the saints "as shorn sheep having put aside the burdens of the world like so much fleece, and as ascending from the washing, which is baptism, all to create twins, which are the two precepts of love, and I see none of them sterile of this holy fruit". Augustine wonders about the pleasure he takes in this figuration as he, like D. W. Robertson, is sure that one does not learn "anything else besides that which he learns when he hears the same thought expressed in plain words". Indeed, whether a figure is used or not

---

[1] *ST*, I.1.10 ad 3, see too *Quodlibet* VII.15 ad 1; see W. J. Ong, "The Province of Rhetoric and Poetry", *The Modern Schoolman*, 19 (1942), 25 quoting *I Posteriorum Analyticorum Aristotelis Expositio*, lect. I; *Aristotle's De Anima . . . and the commentary of St Thomas Aquinas*, tr. K. Foster and S. Humphries (London, 1951), I. sections 107 and 190. Here and on the subject of this chapter in general I was helped by J. Mazzeo, "Dante's Conception of Poetic Expression", *RR*, 47 (1956), 241–58, and "Dante and the Pauline Modes of Vision", *HTR*, 50 (1957), 275–306.
[2] *In Sententias Petri Lombardi Commentaria*, Pr., Ql, a5, ad3, in W. J. Ong, "Wit and Mystery: A Revaluation in Medieval Latin Hymnody", *Spec*, 22 (1947), 324.
[3] *ST*, I.1.9 ad 1; see E. Curtius, *European Literature in the Latin Middle Ages*, tr. W. R. Trask (New York, 1953), 222–5; *Exégèse*, II.2.275 ff.

makes no difference to our cognitive apprehension, "since the thing perceived is the same".[4] Nevertheless, Augustine admits that in the figuration "I contemplate the saints more pleasantly ... it seems sweeter to me than if no such similitude were offered in the divine books." Although cognitively the figuration is a virtually functionless appendix, he finds it mysteriously affecting. This is an unsatisfactory account and could even imply that Augustine is enjoying an unintelligible figurative sweetness in as self-indulgent and mindless a way as all those "romantics" whom Robertson weaves out of his imagination.[5] It might also imply that Aquinas shows greater relevance in demanding that we banish such irrational affective appendages from discourse committed to the pursuit of knowledge. However misleading such suggestions might be, they reflect the confusion in which the problems of justifying figurative expression had been left by Augustine.

The only function of figurative writing in theories which follow Augustine is that it acts like a strangely enjoyable "puzzle" to obscure "something already known"; the puzzle is composed of the "chaff" of figurative expression which conceals the "fruit" of literal discourse or familiar theological propositions. The positive claim for this obfuscation is that "it stimulates a desire to learn, and at the same time excludes those who are unworthy from the mysteries of the faith."[6] But statements like this can only serve to gratify elitist tendencies intrinsic to all cults of an "elect". As for the "chaff" of figurative expression, it is envisaged as a code language concealing "already known" propositions. Such accounts of metaphor and allegory are venerable enough, and J. Pépin has traced the hellenistic antecedents in detail, as well as carefully describing their role in Augustine's allegorical rationale. The whole tradition is convinced that one can express the ideas in question abstractly, although it preferred "to translate them" through fresh images. This "translation" produced an obscurity which was thought to stimulate research.[7] Pépin's choice of the word "traduire" in explaining how the relationship between image and proposition was conceived confirms that allegorical images were understood as naive picture models from which one could read off straightforward, unambiguous propositions about a range of subjects which included theology. Theories like the ones looked at so far in this chapter could only reinforce the

[4] On Christian Doctrine, tr. D. W. Robertson (Library of Liberal Arts, 1958), II.6.7–8 (37–8); see Robertson, Preface to Chaucer, 32–3, 54, 56.

[5] Preface, chapter one, e.g., 14 ff.; this isn't a place to argue about his view of the "romantics" but see in contrast, D. V. Erdman, Blake: Prophet Against Empire (revised edn, 1969), M. D. Paley, Energy and the Imagination (London, 1969); on Wordsworth, C. Clarke, Romantic Paradox (London, 1962).

[6] Preface, 32, 35, 53 and references; see J. Pépin, "S. Augustin et al fonction protreptique de l'allégorie", Recherches Augustiniennes, I (1958), 243–86.

[7] Mythe et Allégorie (Paris, 1958), part III; id., Recherches Augustiniennes, I (1958), 250, 267, 284.

tendencies in figurative writing which have been analysed in the last two chapters—tendencies which find a worthy manifestation in those dictionaries which gave meanings, or translations, of allegorical images.[8]

In expressing this theory of allegory one critical model predominated, and we have already met it on several occasions. It has many variants, as the chaff and the fruit, the rind and the pith, the honeycomb and the honey, the bread and the fragmented bread, but the *genus* to which these belong can be designated the shell and kernel model. Figurative expression is the shell or cortex concealing the discursive kernel which must be extracted by allegorical interpretation, stripping off the figurative shell. The model was so accepted that it controlled thought about Biblical *figura*, from Jerome to the Renaissance. Here the literal or historical dimension is taken as surface shell or cortex while the spiritual (allegorical) meaning is the concealed kernel which must be abstracted.[9] That this model was found as suitable for thinking about the theologians' allegory as the poets' will not surprise us when we recall parts of the discussion in the previous chapter, and de Lubac's opinion that later medieval exegetical work added to the confusion of specifically Christian allegory with other forms of allegory and Philonic moralization, encouraging the treatment of the Bible as a static figurative encyclopaedia.[10] The dominant critical model certainly reflects and reinforces practices of medieval allegory which we have examined, but it cannot help anyone to justify poetry and its figurative procedures against St Thomas's adverse evaluation.

Nevertheless, the model was so deep rooted that even when theorists attempted to meet the objections to poetic *figura*, inevitable whenever the shell-kernel model is confronted by responsible criticism (such as Thomas's), they usually failed to break away from the model which was itself fatal to their cause. Boccaccio is a good example of a writer attempting to defend poetic allegory in the fourteenth century. In his *De Genealogia Deorum Gentilium* he argues that "under a rough shell" the poetic figure hides a knowledge which is "founded upon things eternal and confirmed by original principles". If we pluck away the shell we find a divinely guaranteed truth. This thesis leads Boccaccio into great difficulty. Having

---

[8] We are reminded of Coleridge's comments on allegory as "but a translation of abstract notions into a picture-language", *Lay Sermons*, ed. R. J. White (London, 1972), 30.

[9] Robertson demonstrated the model's prevalence in *Preface*, 54–5, 60, 302–3, 308–9, 316–17 etc; on its exegetical use, Lubac, *Exégèse* I.1.58 n. 3; 127, 286, 308 notes; I.2.403–5, 407, 440, 447, 451, 477–8 notes, 600–3, 609–13; II.1.139, 201, 303, 381; II.2.117, 170–1, 184–6, 190–7, 237–9, etc.

[10] *Exégèse*, II.2.213 (182–214 *passim*): modern typologists usually object to the model, e.g., K. J. Woolcombe, *Essays in Typology*, 54; Hanson, *Allegory and Event*, 25.

maintained the anti-historical case that poetry veils knowledge which is "founded upon things eternal" and that at "all times and places this knowledge is the same, unshaken by any possible change", he is yet forced to judge the pagan poets whom he is defending "as boys ignorant of philosophy or a mountaineer ignorant of navigation, or a man congenitally blind who does not know his letters. Such were the pagan poets." How then does this ignorance "proceed from the bosom of God" whose wisdom can be found beneath the figurative shell? Matters are not improved by emphasizing the standard view that poetry "under the guise of invention, illustrates or proves an idea; and, as its superficial aspect is removed, the meaning of the author is clear."[11] We wonder why, if the question concerns poets whose ignorance of reality is like that of "boys ignorant of philosophy or a mountaineer ignorant of navigation", Boccaccio seduces us to read poetry when by removing the "superficial aspect" of figural expression we only uncover discursive falsity and ignorance—the very sub-rationality about which St Thomas warned. Despite such major problems, Boccaccio concludes optimistically: "If, then, sense is revealed from under the veil of fiction, the composition of fiction is no idle nonsense." But even if we discount the palpable ignorance he attributes to pagan poets, the justification remains specious. Because the discursive kernel makes "sense" it does not necessarily follow that "the composition of fiction" (i.e. the construction which prevents the poem from being simply discursive "sense") is itself "not idle nonsense". It may be a pleasant puzzle but this conventional explanation does not help Boccaccio to escape the charge that poetry and its figurations are, at best, trivial and sub-rational. The weaknesses of his argument are closely related to his critical model, the standard shell-kernel one—poetry "veils truth in a fair and fitting garment" or hides discursive propositions "under a rough shell".[12]

At one point Boccaccio specifically attacks opponents who use the traditional theoretical distinction between the allegory of the theologians and the allegory of the poets:

> My opponents will add that their writings are not fiction but rather figures, to use the correct term, and their authors are figurative writers. O silly subterfuge! As if I were likely to believe that two things to all appearances exactly alike should gain the power of different effects by mere change or difference of name.[13]

Here Boccaccio is explicitly confirming what we have seen in previous chapters: in spite of theoretical differences, the dominant allegorical

---

[11] Osgood's translation in *Boccaccio on Poetry* (Princeton, 1930), XIV.1,4,7,8.
[12] *ibid.*, XIV.1; XIV.7; parallels XIV.12; XIV.18.
[13] *ibid.*, 64–5.

modes of exegetes, preachers and poets showed a great deal in common, sharing figurative practices and models. One must sympathize with his outrage since it is based on correct observation of apparent practices and the common assumption that all figurative writing is best considered in terms of shells and kernels. But his argument comprises no kind of theoretical answer to his opponents objections, and its own unquestioning adherence to the dominant shell-kernel aesthetic could as easily be demonstrating the fatuity of both theologians' allegory and poets' allegory. His passive dependence on the shell-kernel model inhibits his polemic and leaves it at a primitive and superficial stage.[14]

Another early humanist, Salutati, contributed to the debate. In a recent work on Italian humanist thought C. Trinkaus decided that "Salutati's ideas are in complete harmony with the long patristic and medieval traditions of figural interpretation." They are certainly at one with the theories proposed in defence of figurative writing which we have just been analysing.[15] Replying to Giovanni Dominici's attack on poetry, Salutati follows the line that poetry uses figurative expression in the same way as the Bible:

And what is there in the entire body of the sacred volume of the Old Testament (. . .) or even of the New, which the first contains in foreshadowed language [quod primum illud adumbratis sermonibus continebat] (and which is dispersed in four Gospels, the canonic Epistles, the Acts of the Apostles and the Apocalypse remote from understanding), which does not also contain beneath the skin [sub cortice] something other than it shows, and which cannot rightly be called and should be called bilingual?[16]

Once again the shell-kernel model is taken for granted and the historical dynamic between the Old and New Testament tends to be dissolved, for the Old Testament images "contain beneath the skin" precisely what the New Testament contains literally.[17] Salutati

---

[14] For examples of the way Boccaccio assumes figural writing works in practice see IV.44, discussed in chapter one, and on Virgil's *Aeneid*, I and IV, see Boccaccio XIV.13; I don't analyse this here as the mode has been met frequently enough in the last two chapters.

[15] *In our Image and Likeness*, 2 vols. (London, 1969), II.570; see de Lubac, *Exégèse*, II.2.483.

[16] Quoted in Trinkaus, II.569 (Latin text, 875). For Petrarch's similarity, *Familiari* X.4, tr. in J. H. Robinson and H. W. Rolfe, *Petrarch: The First Modern Man of Letters* (London, 1898), see 261–75.

[17] For the view that the OT actually contained the NT as a shell the kernel, and that allegory (manifest through the Incarnation) breaks open this shell see many of the references from de Lubac in note nine of this chapter and see too *Exégèse* I.1. chapter 5 *passim*, I.2.399–400, 499–503, 671–2; II.2.60–72, 81–3, 107 ff., 271–2, 275, etc. That Augustine expounds this tenet to "the uninstructed" in *On the Catechising of the Uninstructed*, IV.8, shows how fundamental it was.

appropriately appeals to Origen and applauds his "pious" and "laudable" exegesis of Genesis because he led all back to a mystical understanding and expounded it in wonderful allegorical senses.[18] Salutati goes on, "Regard the Judaic histories, look at Kings and the rest which follows, are they not all reduced to allegorical comprehension?" These books and the events they record are offered as illustrations of the same figurative mode as the lyrical allegory of the Canticle. Indeed, Salutati asks, "is not the entire Old Testament believed to be the figure and idea of the New?" Without any doubt the figurative relationship between acts, events and total situation in the Old Testament is seen as an example of poetic *figura* or allegory, where the image is an obscured and "cortexed" picture model which we can decode, thus extracting direct information. Salutati demonstrates how this procedure works by expounding Psalm 21. There is no need to repeat his exegesis in detail because the mode and its assumptions will be very familiar by this stage. Christ is referred to in the Psalm as a "worm", according to Salutati: the Psalmist "calls Christ a worm for this reason, just as a worm is not born by seminal generation, so Christ was conceived by no man's semen". He concludes that in the Bible's *figura* everything has "one meaning on the surface and another within [unum in cortice . . . et aliud intrinsecus].[19] The image of the worm is taken as a model from which we are to read off doctrinal propositions, so disposing of the obfuscating cortex which has supposedly spurred us on to find the concealed propositions.

Salutati also finds this mode in the *theologia poetica*—hardly surprising when it is seen as the one common to poets. Thus in *De Laboribus Herculis*, "a mystical interpretation opens up the secrets of the poets." The only difference Salutati sees between theologians' and poets' allegory is that in the Bible both letter and hidden sense are true, whereas in poetry the truth is beneath the skin ("sub cortice") and although the skin may resemble truth it is always fictitious. He applies his principles to understanding poets and sacred history.[20] Confessing belief in the "truth" of a narrative, as we have seen, tends to be something of a red herring, for it may make little difference to the modes, practices or to the theories brought forward to explain the nature, relevance and impact of figurative writing.

Here we can close this brief survey of the dominant models produced to account for figurative expression. It was assumed that poets all employ a parabolic mode in which the full sense of the poem, whatever figurative language it uses, lies only in the discursive

---

[18] In Trinkaus, II.569 (Latin text, 813: "cuncta reducens ad mysticum intellectum mirabilis allegorice sensibus exposuit").

[19] Trinkaus, II.569–71 (Latin texts, 813–4).

[20] Trinkaus, II.700 (Latin text, 866): see 697–704.

referent which Thomas calls "the literal sense".[21] This literal sense is to be extracted from the figurative shell which the poet places round the kernel. Usk, Hawes and Henryson are among the late medieval poets who make their similar assumptions quite clear, and in his book on Lydgate D. A. Pearsall justly states that this critical model was a "cornerstone of medieval aesthetic".[22] The "aesthetic" manifested itself in the practice described over the last two chapters.

Any progression from this sterile circle would have to come from a rather different understanding of the ways in which men can use language to express theological and psychological insights. And, in fact, another approach to allegorical writing did exist in the Middle Ages—an approach which accepted figurative expression as an integral part of the writer's vision. This is far removed from the conception of all figurative expression and images as examples of encoding husks from which we can abstract the discursive (true) kernel, which we already knew in any case. The alternative approach envisaged the image as intrinsic to a whole process of understanding, functioning like Ramsey's "disclosure model" but perhaps going beyond even this in believing that the figurative expression has the irreplacable dimension of Cassirer's "mythical images".[23] It faces the disparity between the region which the figurative writer claims to disclose and the region of empirical tests, controls and daily human discourse by which the disclosure is to be effected. Such images are not taken as picture models from which a series of already articulated propositions are to be drawn; they are, rather, essential parts of a total process. The image becomes functional in important ways as theorists admit that some writers may think with their figures. M. Black has put this idea clearly:

There are powerful and irreplacable uses of metaphor not adequately described by the old formula of "saying one thing and

---

[21] Besides texts in first three notes of this chapter, *Quodlibet*, VII.6.3 ad 2; see also J. Chydenius, "The Theory of Medieval Symbolism", *CHR*, 27 (1960), 37–8.

[22] Pearsall, *Lydgate*, 193–5; for Lydgate see "The Church and The Bird", 11.1–7, 15–16, 30 in *The Minor Poems*, EETS, 192 (1933); II.468–9; Hawes, *Pastime of Pleasure*, EETS, 173 (1927), 11. 36–42, 50–6, 716–21; Henryson, *Fables*, 11. 15–18 and *Orpheus and Eurydice*, 11.419–20; Usk, prologue and conclusion to *Testament of Love* in *Chaucerian and Other Pieces*, ed. W. W. Skeat (Oxford, 1897).

[23] In his *Language and Myth*, tr. S. K. Langer (Dover books edn), 37–8, 56–7, etc., and *Mythical Thought*, tr. R. Manheim (New Haven, 1968), Introduction, Part I (especially 38–9) and IV: I'm aware that his account of myth in early society is taken to be seriously misguided (see Kirk, *Myth: its meaning and functions in ancient and other cultures* (Cambridge, 1970), 238–51 and chapter VI), but his work provides some relevant models here. To the approach I'm describing, the traditional theory of "accommodation" is related: see K. Gründer, *Figur und Geschichte* (Munich, 1958), chapter II; Patrides, *TSLL*, 5 (1963), 58 ff.

meaning another". A memorable metaphor has the power to bring separate domains into cognitive and emotional relation by using language directly appropriate to the one as a lens for seeing the other. . . . Metaphorical thought, is a distinctive mode of achieving insight, not to be construed as an ornamental substitute for plain thought.[24]

It is this approach, so congenial to much modern criticism, which provides the hints towards one resolution of the problems raised in this chapter, although it is certainly a mistake to try and apply it indiscriminately to the dominant medieval figural practices and critical models, as the preceding two and half chapters have shown.[25]

The alternative theory I have been sketching out is articulated in the *Letter to Can Grande*, generally accepted as Dante's.[26] The final purpose of the *Commedia*, he writes, "is to remove those living in this life from a state of misery, and bring them to a state of happiness". This was also the final aim of the Bible which, as Nicholas of Lyra said, "is the book of life in that it is the instrument for attaining true or blessed life".[27] And yet, as Mazzeo has shrewdly noticed, Dante does not tell us that his "fictive" form is a cortex enwrapping an already familiar and known truth which one could express as well in literalistic discourse.[28] In section nineteen of the *Letter* Dante discusses the invocation of the *Paradiso*. He points out that the poet "will tell of those things which he was able to retain in his mind". This is not a casual reference to the poet's inadequate training in the fifth and mnemonic part of the preparation of his oration. Rather it suggests the "uncommon nature" of the "sublime matters" which the poet has undertaken, and the shortcomings of our cognitional capacities in attempting to apprehend them. Nonetheless the poet Dante *has* been able to retain at least part of his vision and it is this which he purposes to manifest, a vision "concerning the celestial kingdom whatsoever he was able to store up, like a treasure in his mind".[29] He does not assert that in his poem or in his mind there is a treasure which consists of discursive propositions that can be

---

[24] *Models and Metaphors* (New York, 1962), 236–7.
[25] Black's statement of course has much in common with claims about the "unparaphrasable" nature of medieval and renaissance allegory mentioned in my Introduction: how inappropriate such claims are to dominant modes, I hope I have shown.
[26] *The Letter* is quoted from *Dantis Alagherii Epistolae*, text and tr. P. Toynbee (Oxford, 1920): concerning the letter's authenticity, see Charity, *Events and their Afterlife* (Cambridge, 1966), 199–200 and references, and the discussion of its significance, 199–213; de Lubac's discussion is also relevant, *Exégèse*, II.2.321–4, as is A. D. Nuttall, *Two Concepts of Allegory* (London, 1967), chapter two.
[27] *Letter*, 202 (178).
[28] "Dante's Concept of Poetic Expression", *RR*, 47 (1956), 252: an important article.
[29] *Letter*, 204.

extracted (like a kernel) from a cryptographic picturing model which we perceive. That Dante should here omit such a revered and hoary critical model in the explanation of the mode of poetry which is avowedly "fictivus" is important in itself. The subject is one which he can only think about seriously and sustainedly in figures, searching for apt "disclosure models", while continually aware that:

> On a huge hill
> Cragged, and steep, Truth stands, and hee that will
> Reach her, about must, and about must goe;
> > Donne, *Satyres* III.79–81

But section nineteen also reminds the reader that if Dante could attain and re-create the experience and the vision through his journey, others may be able to do likewise.[30] This approach is stressed and further clarified in sections 28 and 29 of the *Letter*. Dante likens himself, the poet, to the visionary St Paul "caught up to the third heaven", to the Prophet Ezekiel confronted with "the likeness of the glory of the Lord", and to the three Disciples falling on their faces at the Transfiguration of Christ and the voice out of the bright cloud. In the vision, Dante writes, the human intellect "reaches such a height of exaltation that after its return to itself memory fails, since it has transcended the range of human faculty [propter transcendisse humanum modum]." What was disclosed in the intellectual vision is seen to be outside the normal range of human reason and so, "non recordabatur". In all the visionary instances he cites, he notices the failure of memory.[31] Even where memory may manage to hold the insight, power of speech fails ("sermo tamen deficit"). This leads into a comment which contrasts strikingly with Thomas's attitude to Plato's use of myth and figure:

> For we perceive many things by the intellect for which language has no terms—a fact which Plato indicates plainly enough in his books by his employment of metaphors, for he perceived many things by the light of the intellect which his everyday language was inadequate to express.[32]

Whereas St Thomas maintained that poetic figure was used to conceal an absence of truth, in Dante's view it is conventional discourse and direct statement which are deficient ("sermo tamen deficit"): unlike Thomas, he believed that Plato perceived much that direct language was unable to express. For Dante, the vision and its insights cannot

---

[30] *Letter*, 204 (181): see Charity's comments on this passage in *Events*, 236.
[31] *Letter*, section 28 (2 Corinthians 13.2–4, etc.).
[32] *Letter*, section 29, 209–10 (193)

simply be replaced by non-figural writing. To meet the reader's natural scepticism about his claims, Dante refers to the mystical writings and experience of Richard of St Victor, St Bernard and St Augustine. Richard's work meditates on this problem, admitting that what the visionary saw before in truth and clarity he cannot recall in any completeness, for he now sees as if through a veil or in the middle of a cloud, and in an astonishing way remembering does not remember, seeing does not behold ("mirum in modum reminis-centes non reminiscimur, dum videntes non pervidemus . . .").[33] The image of veil and cloud suggest the state of mind trying to re-create and regain the disclosure in the very act of expression. It is em-phatically not the veil of Boccaccio or his fellow theorists, where the veil is an obfuscating and seductive cortex designed to make a picturing model a little more interesting. The Paradiso itself touches on these ideas:

> O divina virtù, se mi ti presti
> tanto che l'ombra del beato regno
> segnata nel mio capo io manifesti

(O power divine, if thou grant me so much of thyself that I may show forth the shadow of the blessed kingdom imprinted in my brain) *Paradiso* I.22–4[34]

And later Beatrice in resolving one of Dante's doubts explains the mode of vision available to men:

> Così parlar conviensi al vostro ingegno,
> però che solo da sensato apprende
> ciò che fa poscia d'intelletto degno.
> Per questo la Scrittura condescende
> a vostra facultate, e piedi e mano
> attribuisce a Dio, ed altro intende:
> e Santa Chiesa con aspetto umano
> Gabrïel e Michel vi rappresenta,
> e l'altro che Tobia refece sano.

(It is necessary to speak thus to your faculty, since only from sense perception does it grasp that which it then makes fit for the intellect. For this reason Scripture condescends to your capacity and attributes hands and feet to God, having another meaning, and Holy Church represents to you with human aspect Gabriel and

---

[33] *Benjamin Minor*, IV.23 quoted by Toynbee, 191 n. 4; see Mazzeo, *RR*, 47 (1956), 252, 255.
[34] The text and translation here and below is from *The Divine Comedy*, ed. and tr. J. D. Sinclair, 3 vols. (Oxford UP paperback, 1971).

Michael and the other who made Tobit whole again.) *Paradiso*
iv.40–8

Thus the poet labours to recall and deliver his vision in words. The
poem calls the reader to participate in a process whose totality is the
vision the writer has won back in the action of composition.
Through this process the religious poet hopes "to remove those living
in this life from a state of misery, and to bring them to a state of
happiness".[35]

The understanding of language and the function of figurative
expression and imagery just described is obviously distinct from the
one which dominated medieval poetics and exegetical practice. Here
the puzzling questions evaded by Augustine and his successors,
together with the challenge made by St Thomas and others to the
status of figurative poetry, meet the best response orthodox Christianity offers. And if this is the case, then a modern critic would
commit a great folly either to ignore this line of thought or to try and
force it into the standard shell-kernel aesthetic. Furthermore, the
approach to religious thinking and experience here implies a different
kind of writing from any we have considered so far in exegesis,
preaching or literary allegory. It points to a work where a writer will
consciously attempt to create a "disclosure model" which cannot be
confused with picture models, one in which the poetic process and
its imagistic organization is integral to the poet's exploration and
vision. The remainder of the present book should establish that *Piers
Plowman* is just such a work. In his own development of allegorical
modes Langland also perceived the underlying theory of the
theologians' allegory and used it to help him manifest his own vision
—despite its manifold tension and perplexities, an essentially
orthodox Christian vision. The theologians' allegory was one of the
ways of thinking about Christianity, and however ossified it had
become by Langland's time its conceptual structure did retain some
hints towards meditating and talking about sacred history in relation
to Christ's acts, time present and the individual writer's situation—
hints which focus on images and events in the generation of vision.
This is not to deny that Langland uses picture models as well, but
it does mean a critic must be awake to the possibility of kinds of
figurative models other than those we have been mainly concerned
with so far; in a different kind of figurative process even picture
models could possibly serve more than a trivial function, while
still remaining within an orthodox framework.

Langland himself most explicitly gives some indication of his
views on these problems at the opening of the twelfth passus of *Piers*

---

[35] *Letter*, section 15.

Plowman (B-text). Ymagynatyf, "idel was I neuere", fittingly summons up the images of Will's past life and perilous future.[36] One
of the charges against Will is, "thow medlest the with makynges and
myȝtest go sey thi sauter" (XII.16). It is typical of Langland to raise
this issue seriously and in genuine self-questioning. It is equally
typical that he does not take any of the glib evasions encouraged by
a shell-kernel theory. He does not plead that beneath a false but
enjoyable cortex he presents a kernel of discursive truth, nor does he
plead that if only we see his cryptographic picture model aright, we
will be able to read off various, necessary, and true propositions.
This omission is certainly worthy of attention, as it was in Dante's
Letter. That a writer does *not* use a received and venerated theory and
critical model, or does *not* exploit the standard polemical justifications
is important evidence of his own position. Will accepts the charge
("I seight well he sayde me soth"). His "excuse" is interesting:

> "Catoun conforted his sone that, clerke though he were
> To solacen hym sum tyme as I do whan I make;
> . . .
> And of holy men I herde," quod I "How thei other-while
> Pleyden the parfiter to be in many places."
>
> (XII.21-2; 24-5)

Here we will note the words *tyme, make, pleyden*, though their implications are only fully illuminated by Langland's thinking with them in
other contexts which I shall consider below. He goes on to face
Ymagynatif's objection that there are numerous homiletic writings
and preachers to instruct men "what Dowel is Dobet, and Dobet
bothe" (XII.17-19). Again he makes no general reply but only an
extremely personal one:

> Ac if there were any wight that wolde me telle
> What were Dowel and Dobet and Dobest atte laste,
> Wolde I neuere do werke but wende to holicherche,
> And there bydde my bedes but whan ich eet or slepe.
>
> (XII.26-9)

All these homilies and preachers cannot serve to resolve the doubts
of the individual writer: Will's poetry is part of his "werke", part
of his search for a total vision. And if Langland saw his writing in the

---

[36] All quotations and references are to the B-test unless otherwise stated; I
have eliminated Skeat's medial point. Elizabeth Kirk also discusses Langland on
poetry in her book, *The Dream Thought of Piers Plowman* (New Haven, 1972),
77-8, 140-5; on "Ymagynatyf" see two articles, R. Quirk, *JEGP*, 53 (1954),
81-3, H. S. V. Jones, *JEGP*, 13 (1914), 583-8, and M. W. Bloomfield, *Piers
Plowman*, 170-4.

way I maintain, he probably realized that with his questionings he could only cease writing at the final Apocalypse, when the vision would be achieved "face to face".[37] Until then he can only glimpse the vision, and the glimpse reinspires the "werks" of exploration and the writing of poetry so inextricably bound up with it—for Langland:

> "Bi Cryste," quod Conscience tho, "I wil bicome a pilgryme,
> And walken as wyde as al the worlde lasteth,
> To seke Piers the Plowman . . .
> . . .
> And sitthe he gradde after grace til I gan awake."
>> (XX.378–80; 384)

The function of poetry envisaged seems to be much closer to one found in the *Letter to Can Grande* than to the dominant shell-kernel aesthetic.

I singled out Langland's choice of the word "make" to describe his writing. This would not demand comment in itself, for the word was hardly an uncommon one for poeticizing.[38] But Langland's use of "make" gains more profound implications through two other contexts in which he employs it. In the magnificent confession of faith in Passus V (V.485–513), Repentance speaks of:

> al that Marke hath ymade Mathew, Iohan, and Lucas,
> Of thyne douȝtiest dedes were don in owre armes;
>> (V.507–8)

Langland then, is like the Evangelists; all are "makers". Langland has "ymade" much from his own searchings as well as from Christ's "douȝtiest dedes"; these deeds are both the centre of his search, and the centre of the poem, while Christ is hero of both. Christ's role is more germane to chapter five, but it is relevant here in helping us to focus on Langland's understanding of his activity as poet or maker, for he uses figurative expression in a way which matches this understanding. Not only have the evangelists "ymade", but so has the Creator, who:

> is a creatour of all kynnes thinges
> Fader and fourmour of all that euere was maked;
> And that is the gret god that gynnynge had neuere,
>> (IX.26–8)

---

[37] 1 Corinthians 13.12.
[38] See Skeat's note to V.507–8; for instance, Lydgate, "Fall of Princes", *EETS*, 121 (1924), I.11.250, 356 (7,10).

And "all the euere was maked", the great Artificer made through his own word:

> For thorugh the worde that he spake wexen forth bestes,
>> Dixit, et facta sunt:
>
> And made man likkest to hym-self one,
>
>> (IX.32–3)

When God says "faciamus" (Gen. 1.26), it is:

> As who seith, more mote here-to than my worde one;
> My3te mote help now with my speche".
>
>> (IX.36–7)

God creates through "my3te", "worde" and "werkemanschip" (IX.25–47). As the Good Samaritan himself says:

> So is the fader a ful god formeour and shepper,
>> Tu fabricator omnium, etc.,
>
> And al the my3te myd hym is in makyng of thynges.
>> (XVII.167–8)

There is thus a rich matrix of meaning round Langland's perception of himself as a maker. No such implications could be developed among the shell and kernel theorists or practitioners.

Langland's own activity in these relations is touched on in another passage. Here he brings together two other words I singled out earlier —"tyme" and "pleyden"—in conjunction with notions about verbalizing. Wit explains to Will that he does best who:

> with-draweth hym by day and bi ny3te
> To spille any speche or any space of tyme;
>> (IX.96–7)

He warns the poet Will:

> Lesyng of tyme treuthe wote the sothe!
> Is moste yhated vp erthe of hem that beth in heuene,
> And sitthe to spille speche that spyre is of grace,
> And goddes gleman and a game of heuene;
> Wolde neuere the faithful fader his fithel were vntempred,
> Ne his gleman a gedelynge a goer to tauernes!
>> (IX.98–102)

There are a number of things to notice in this evocative passage. "Speche" and "tyme" are most highly valued and linked. (Speech, language, is not here the sugared husk concealing plain discursive meaning.) We immediately see how crucial is Ymagynatyf's charge, implying that Will's "makynges" are a waste of *time*, a waste which is most odious to those in heaven. But we also notice that "makynges" will be doubly heinous if they also "spille speche", because of the great potential of "speche" as "spyre of grace". We have already heard God making men and beasts in *his* "speche", and Passus XVIII tells us that the Virgin "conceyued thorw speche / And grace of the holy goste" (129–30). So the repercussions of "spille speche" are indeed wide. Furthermore, the potential of speech is associated with the other word I underlined in Passus XII—"pleyden". Here (IX) speech becomes "a game of heuene", while in XII.25 Will thinks holy men, "Pleyden the parfiter to be". For Langland the play, the game, is a saving game, and its medium is speech, particularly the remembering and creating speech of the makers.[39] At the centre of the game are the "douȝtiest dedes" of the Word, while the human poet whose medium is "makynges" in "speche that spyre is of grace", could be God's "fithel" and his "gleman". He could be God's "fithel" because the poet's vision manifested in words, also delivers God's own "speche" and word / Word; so the four Evangelists "ymade . . . Of thyne douȝtiest dedes", making the Gospels as poets disclosing a vision.

With this conception of the poet-*vates* there is the strong possibility of parody. Abusers of speech and time are common and they tend to appear in *Piers Plowman* as false minstrels.[40] Particularly relevant here is Studye's complaint about those deceivers who "speke foule wordes", abuse their own and others' lives, and:

> conne namore mynstralcye na musyke, men to glade,
> Than Munde the mylnere of *multa fecit deus!*
>
> (X.43–4; see 38–44)

The poet of *Piers Plowman*, so conscious of the potential of speech, has to decide whether he himself is maker or anti-maker, one of the *vates* or a grotesque parody of these.

That such considerations arise from Langland's thought about the poet's role as maker, confirms my emphasis on the disparity between

---

[39] The wealth of meaning in Middle English "game" is discussed by V. A. Kolve, *The Play Called Corpus Christi* (London, 1966), chapter two: there's also a classic study by J. Huizinga, *Homo Ludens* (Paladin paperback), see especially chapter VII.

[40] E. T. Donaldson has an excellent discussion of Langland's minstrels in his *Piers Plowman* (London, 1966), 136–54.

his approach to the problems discussed in this chapter and the approach of the proponents of shell-kernel aesthetics. We should again stress that the latters' theory and critical model did indeed dominate medieval thought about language, figure and poetry. Nevertheless we have found another line of thought available and that Langland's own suggestive ideas on these problems should be seen in relation to Dante's *Letter* and this alternative theory of "making". It will be possible, therefore, to approach *Piers Plowman* in chapter five with the knowledge that Langland may well have realized his thinking in kinds of figurative writing and in poetic models which are not reducible either to the dominant modes of medieval figurative writing or to the dominant models of medieval critical theory. Here "historical critics" should not assume that the outstanding thinkers and poets of an age will necessarily be fully representative and typical of the dominant assumptions of an age.[41]

I conclude this chapter by juxtaposing three passages in *Piers Plowman* and one in Augustine's work. These passages are relevant to the arguments I have offered about Langland's understanding of the possibilities of figurative expression which, when extended, is usually called allegory. In a famous image in the fifth Passus Piers tells the pilgrims that if they follow the way he has abstracted for them, then each one:

> shalt see in thi-selue Treuthe sitte in thine herte,
> In a cheyne of charyte
>
> (V.615–6)[42]

Much later in the poem the ever inquiring Will is searching out Charity, and in a dialogue with Anima we suddenly find the "he" which referred to "Charite" now becomes Christ. Will comments:

> Clerkis kenne me that cryst is in alle places;
> Ac I seygh hym neuere sothly but as my-self in a miroure,
> *Ita in enigmate, tunc facie ad faciem.*
>
> (XV.156–7; see 145–65)

Thus Will's movement through introspection towards Christ is brought into meaningful relation with the first figure I quoted from Piers's instructions in Passus V; *now* the figure is personalized, and it has been realized as part of a process. It will be noticed the vision

---

[41] See Q. Skinner, "The limitations of Historical Explanation", *Philosophy*, 41 (1966), 212–14: his arguments developed in "Meaning and Understanding in the History of Ideas", *History and Theory*, 8, (1969), 3–53.

[42] On the chain of charity, Elizabeth Zeeman (Salter), "Piers Plowman and the Pilgrimage to Truth", *ES*, 11 (1958), 1–16.

"in enigmate" has nothing to do with the enigmatic cortex of the shell-kernel aesthetic. The vision will deepen and the historic-dimension (as we shall see in the next chapter) has to be re-created, but the models already offered in these two brief passages are far removed from the picture models which dominated exegesis, homiletic and literary allegory. The other passage from *Piers Plowman* is in Passus seventeen of the C-text. Will makes a comment which may round off these arguments. He describes how he can find true Charity nowhere, and concludes:

> And thow finde hym bote figuratifliche a ferly me thinketh;
> *Hic in enigmate, tunc facie ad faciem:*
>
> (C XVII.294)

This kind of figure, searched for by Will and the poet, again bears no resemblance to the picturing models we have explored. The poet, and his Will, is like the reader in that he can now "fynde hym bote figuratifliche". But although fallen back into introspection and memory, "in enigmate", the poet *has* achieved the vision and his labour is to re-create both the insight and the process of insight, in which the "cosmic disclosure" is realized. In the re-creation he too will be thinking "figuratifliche", and will be guiding inquisitor of models and images, trying to disclose to us the "ferly" he perceived, and continually attempting to clarify the perception by the very act of writing.

The passage from St Augustine links closely with the two pieces just taken from *Piers Plowman*; Augustine is drawing to the close of his major work on the Trinity, and speculates that "when the vision 'face to face' shall come", we shall see the Trinity more clearly "than we now see its image which we are". He then counsels men to

> look upon their mind as an image, so that they are able in some way or other to refer what they see to Him, whose image it is, and also to see by conjecturing that which they now see through the image by beholding, since they cannot yet see face to face. For . . . "we now see through a mirror".[43]

This is the kind of thinking which, I have argued is exploited and certainly understood by Dante and Langland. It leads our ideas away from the assumptions and models of the shell-kernel aesthetics and leads us towards "disclosure models" and the re-creation of the process of insight through an exploration in necessarily "figuratif"

---

[43] *On the Trinity*, XV.23.44; see G. B. Ladner, *The Idea of Reform* (Cambridge, Mass., 1959), chapter 5, section 3.

discourse, with the possibility of participation in the culminating vision.

It is well to close this chapter with some comments by William Blake on his own work, which are as apposite as those of Coleridge with which I headed this chapter:

> The Nature of Visionary Fancy or Imagination, is very little known, and the Eternal nature and permanence of its ever Existent Images is consider'd as less permanent than the things of Vegetative and Generative Nature; yet the Oak dies as well as the Lettuce, but Its Eternal Image and Individuality never dies but renews by its seed; just so the Imaginative Image returns by the seed of Contemplative Thought; the Writings of the Prophets illustrate these conceptions of the Visionary Fancy by their various sublime and Divine Images as seen in the Worlds of Vision.[44]

---

[44] Quoted from Blake: *Complete Writings* ed. G. Keynes (London, 1966), 605, without Blake's deletions noted by Keynes.

5 Piers Plowman: Allegorical Modes and Visionary Organization

A Lance he bore, and underneath one arm
A Stone; and in the opposite hand, a Shell
Of a surpassing brightness. Much rejoic'd
The dreaming Man that he should have a Guide
To lead him through the Desert;
Wordsworth, *Prelude* (1805), V.79–83

Because he kept the Divine Vision in time of trouble.
Blake, *Jerusalem* Pl.95

I

Scholarly work on *Piers Plowman* usually reflects the controversy and confusion discussed in the first chapter of this book. Here again interpretation flows between poles represented by D. W. Robertson and his opponents. Characteristically, Robertson and Huppé maintain that *Piers Plowman* has an "allegorical meaning" whose "ultimate source" is in the "nexus of traditional interpretation" around the poet's Biblical quotations. This nexus is to be found in "Biblical exegesis" and allegorical dictionaries.[1] When the poet does not quote from the Bible and the interpreters are having difficulties, they still believe the same nexus is relevant: "When a portion of the poem contained no Biblical text and could not be understood entirely from its context, we attempted to ascertain its Biblical milieu through the use of a concordance or of a *Repertoire exégètique* such as the *Allegoriae in universam sacram scripturam*." They are confident that "homiletic literature" and *Piers Plowman* are alike, "derivatives from the exegetical tradition".[2] But their method begs a host of questions. For instance, what is the relation between an "ultimate source" of a poem's "allegorical meaning" and the poem's own allegorical meaning? What exactly do the authors mean when

---

[1] Robertson and Huppé, *Piers Plowman and Scriptural Tradition* (Princeton. 1951), 2, 5–6.
[2] *ibid.*, 16.

they talk of having understood poetry "entirely" and what criteria are they laying down for determining when a passage has not been "understood entirely from its context"? They assume the way to reach this (still undefined) entire understanding in every case where our apprehension is troubled, must be through conjecturing a "Biblical milieu", then applying the allegorical dictionary to that milieu, and finally feeding the answer back into *Piers Plowman*. Although they do not explain their notion of entire understanding, it becomes clear that it is based on the demand for *all* poetry to be taken as a collection of picture models. They set out to imitate the exegetes' way of reading, which I illustrated at some length, and despite the limitations of naive picture models they have *a priori* certainty that Langland could not have added anything to exegetical and homiletic practice.

We can clarify Robertson and Huppé's position a little more. They maintain that "the basic structure of *Piers Plowman* rests on contrasts which . . . are largely dependent upon an understanding of the application of the traditional levels of meaning." This can be tabulated by critics.[3] First a reader is to decide when a section of the poem is not "understood entirely"; then he must select a "Biblical milieu"; next he discovers how medieval exegetes read this milieu and its images; finally he is to apply these exegetical readings to the poem's context and the images in question, presenting this as the correct understanding of the poetry. This is their method as they outline it, and here are some examples of the way the scholars select "Biblical milieu":

> . . . may have been suggested by . . . (23)
> . . . was probably suggested by . . . (23)
> . . . were probably suggested by . . . (54)
> . . . perhaps suggested to the poet by . . . (79)
> The attitude here expressed recalls . . . (86; see 83–9)
> The poet may have in mind . . . (159)
> The poet probably also had in mind . . . (160)

Having made this risky and rather arbitrary leap they then impose the exegetes' readings and methods onto Langland's images and contexts. Given this procedure it is hardly surprising that Robertson and Huppé find Langland's figurative modes amazingly similar to those of exegetes and homilists.

Another critic who asserts that Langland and the exegetes shared one "allegorical method" is D. C. Fowler; yet his statements about Biblical exegesis in relation to *Piers Plowman* are made without any

---

[3] *ibid.*, 236: page references follow in the text.

apparent knowledge of the theology or practice of the former.[4] Discussing Passus XVI.1–89(B-text), he says that Langland writes "a simultaneous dramatization on the four levels of meaning in scriptural tradition". The subject, Fowler believes, is the Fall. But he then argues that the tree in Passus XVI "is not, of course, the literal tree we find in the Garden of Eden. The poet assumes we have the literal tree in mind." He also claims that although the passage dramatizes traditional fourfold exegesis of the Fall, the role of Piers and the agricultural terms are "imagery, not allegory".[5] It ceases to be at all clear that Fowler's theory has anything "traditional" or even four-levelled about it. He does state that Piers expounded the tree's meaning "on the tropological and allegorical levels", but there could be no allegory in the "traditional" *theory* of the four senses without a literal, historical base. Furthermore, Fowler makes no differentiation between theory and practice, and gives no examples of traditional exegesis, even on Genesis 2 and 3. He tabulates Passus XVI. 73–89 according to four levels "simultaneously" dramatized. But this turns out to be sequential, not simultaneous, and the Incarnation comes in his "Anagogical" column, while the literal level is still only "in mind".[6] Such confusion is typical of literary critics who assert a connection between exegesis and poetry without adequate analysis of exegetical theory or practice. Placing a reference to the Incarnation in the anagogic column not only declares a basic misunderstanding of the simplest "mechanics" of exegesis; far more seriously it involves a complete ignorance of the historical and theological dynamics to which the four senses should, in theory, only be a terse and formulaic kind of reference.

Staying with the Robertsonians, Ben Smith not long ago said that "[Robertson and Huppé's book] demonstrates, I believe, the validity of the exegetical approach for *Piers*." His own book "will constitute an additional defence of the exegetical approach by further demonstrating its effectiveness".[7] Unfortunately Smith's admiration for Robertson and Huppé prevents him from seeing the need to sort out or even clarify the unexamined methodological problems of their book on *Piers Plowman*. Like Fowler, he talks of "the exegetical approach" without stating whether he means the theory or practice of exegesis. It seems he means practice of the kind I have analysed, for even where the poem suggests no scriptural reference he centres his own exegesis of *Piers Plowman* on "the medieval dictionaries and

---

[4] Fowler, *Piers Plowman* (Seattle, 1961), 120–9, 144; see Bloomfield's review in *Spec*, 37 (1962), 120–3.
[5] *ibid.*, 120–2.
[6] *ibid.*, 124–5; some examples of exegesis of Genesis offered in chapter two above.
[7] Smith, *Traditional Imagery of Charity in Piers Plowman* (The Hague, 1966), 12, 14.

compendia of biblical symbols". Once more, it is not surprising that from an explicitly Robertsonian method he constantly finds such "patterns" of meaning in the poem as are "the stock-in-trade of the medieval Christian culture which produced Piers".[8] My own analysis will cast some doubts on whether Langland's figurative practices are quite so "stock-in-trade", but it is certainly a pity that Smith did not scrutinize Robertson's methodology, for we have seen that it is a weak foundation on which to build an interpretative system.[9]

Inevitably the opposition to this school has not remained silent. R. W. Frank viewed Piers Plowman as "a literal rather than an allegorical poem", in which if the poet ever intends "a second meaning . . . he makes it quite obvious . . . and he usually explains his second meaning to us". Piers Plowman is a "personification-allegory" and, Frank insists, "there is not the slightest excuse for decking out a personification-allegory in the mystic garments of medieval scriptural exegesis."[10] However we have found that there need be very few "mystic garments" about the practice of scriptural exegesis—in fact, the exegetes were as explicit in reading off any "second meaning" as Frank believes Langland to be. Nor did the exegetes deny that most of the Bible was "primarily literal"—as we saw, "fundamentum historiae" was a cliché of exegetical theory. To add to the complications in Frank's position, he admits that Langland himself, at least once, wrote a "symbol allegory".[11] As we attempt to disentangle Frank's assumptions we may remember how Rosemond Tuve argued that the term "personification-allegory . . . is especially useless to make the needed discriminations", and it is difficult not to agree with her.[12]

The claims of Robertsonian critics have also been challenged by J. Lawlor. According to him one of the difficulties about applying the exegetical method recommended by Robertson and his followers is that Piers Plowman has a "strikingly literal" form. But in theory this is hardly a problem, for few things could appear more "strikingly literal" than some of the historical narrative exegetes and preachers read allegorically, as examples in our second and third chapter revealed. Another of Lawlor's objections is that,

> Piers Plowman belongs to that type of allegorical work which proceeds by way of personifications of abstracts to the unravelling of problems which press upon man in this life. . . . We may there-

---

[8] ibid., 19–20, 89.
[9] It's also noticeable that Smith unites all medieval figurative theory and practice into one category, "the exegetical"—no nuances appear.
[10] Frank, Piers Plowman and the Scheme of Salvation (New Haven, 1957), 2–3, 8.
[11] ibid., 89.
[12] Allegorical Imagery (Princeton, 1966), 177 n. 17, and see 25 ff.

fore avail ourselves of a useful distinction by following one critic
in calling *Piers Plowman* a "personification-allegory", provided
we allow for the play of accepted symbol and figurative usage
within the general framework. Whatever the case for application
of a fourfold method of interpretation to other kinds of allegory,
it is weakest for personification-allegory. As Dr Frank observes,
"its literal nature renders it an impossible medium for the
fourfold method."

Thus we have two categories: "truly allegorical work" and "personification-allegory". Dante exemplifies the former, Langland the
latter. A distinction Miss Tuve found "especially useless" for
studying "allegorical imagery", Lawlor claims is "useful". But it is
difficult to see that Lawlor produces any evidence to prove Frank's
categories at all "useful", or that he deals with the problems which
Frank left unexamined. Lawlor does seem partially aware of such
problems, since he includes in his category of "personification-
allegory", "the play of accepted symbol and figurative usage". But
this is exactly what Robertson and Huppé think they are elucidating
in their study of *Piers Plowman* and what leads them to the exegetes.
Lawlor's attempt to employ Frank's classifications (with only slight
qualification) in polemic against the Robertsonians, seems to be
quite as unpromising as Frank's own polemic. It also leads him to
those questionable assumptions about the inapplicability of exegetical
methods to writing of a seemingly "literal nature". Furthermore, it
encourages him to follow Frank in asserting that "in the later Middle
Ages the tendency appears to have been decisively away from figurative intepretation".[13] We have discovered the uselessness and
inaccuracy of such generalizations for any study of the questions at
issue (chapters two-four), and these are the chief lines taken by the
opposition to Robertson and his followers.

It is worth driving home the extent and complexity of the confusion in this area of *Piers Plowman* scholarship by examining a passage
from the writing of one of Robertson's most eminent opponents. In
his book on *Piers Plowman* E. T. Donaldson claims that "Piers in his
epiphany as C's Do-Well may, in the anagogical sense, stand for the
prophets who waited patiently for the coming of Christ."[14] But even
if this interpretation were acceptable, the sense could not be
"anagogical". The anagogical sense is based on the Christian notion
of the consummation of the ages, "when Christ will appear in his
glory and come to claim his own to take them with him: such is the
reference of the anagogical sense." It is an eschatological sense. But

[13] Lawlor, *Piers Plowman: An Essay in Criticism* (London, 1962), 251–4 *passim*.
[14] *Piers Plowman: The C-Text and Its Poet* (reprint, London, 1966), 180.

Donaldson is talking about time before the first coming of Christ in his redemptive work, the object of allegory, not anagogy.[15] The question does not merely concern a terminological quibble: the point is that a member of the "opposition" shows that he is unfamiliar with the theology of the four senses and therefore with any potential which their theoretical organization may hold. It is also noticeable that none of Robertson's opponents distinguish between the possible effects of the practice of exegesis and the potential of aspects in its theory: their comments on the issues certainly seem to lack specificity.

In this blurred controversy, Elizabeth Salter made an important observation which is an essential basis for any attempt to understand the kinds of figurative expression in Piers Plowman. She pointed out that Langland's poem "proceeds by a succession of different allegorical modes, working changeably":

> We should be sceptical of critics who recommend to us one kind of allegorical writing as "characteristic" of Piers Plowman. . . . In fact, a whole spectrum of allegorical modes is characteristic of the poem: it displays almost every type of allegory known to the medieval period.[16]

Bearing this in mind, we have attempted to ascertain what theories of figurative imagery were available and what their potential might be, as well as establishing, by close analysis, what the dominant figurative procedures were in practice, and how they handled the ideas and experience they were supposed to articulate. Having studied the theory and practice of exegetical and related allegorical modes we should be especially sensitive to Elizabeth Salter's warning, and show considerable scepticism towards any criticism which implies a one-dimensional relationship between Langland's "allegory" and the exegetes' "allegory". I should make it clear that I am not offering an overall "interpretation" of Piers Plowman. I undertake an analysis of some of the poem's figurative modes and their interrelations, exploiting the discussion and vocabulary of the preceding chapters. Considering some important passages in this way, alongside current criticism, inevitably leads to interpretations, but the more general aim of my exploration is to offer a sound foundation and a model for reading Piers Plowman.

---

[15] I'm translating de Lubac, Exégèse, I.2.621: see chapters eight and ten of this volume.
[16] Piers Plowman, ed. Salter and Pearsall (London, 1967), 3, 8–9, and see Elizabeth Salter, Piers Plowman: An introduction (Oxford, 1962), 66, 78, and Elizabeth Kirk, The Dream Thought of Piers Plowman (New Haven, 1972), 10.

II

In most of the passages I intend to examine, Piers himself is central, and it may be useful to sum up the way scholars have understood this figure. They have certainly found him a veritable Proteus:

Piers "is an eschatological figure" who "stands for satisfaction".[17]

Piers "is St Peter", and "in the last Passus and Dobet is unmistakably Christ".[18]

Piers moves from being "a simple honest labourer" to a point where, "Piers stands for God the Father."[19]

Piers develops from being the "animal" man to being "the spiritual".[20]

Piers "is the model for all owners of property" and also a "symbol for the human nature of Christ".[21]

Piers "represents the infinite".[22]

Piers "represents God's ministry on earth in the status praelatorum", while he also "is the ideal, actualized in Christ".[23]

Piers "personifies Grace".[24]

Piers "is also the Son of God".[25]

Piers's function in the poem "is equivalent to that of the Bride of Christ in Bernard's sermons on the Canticle of Canticles, or in many other commentaries on the Canticles", and he is always "God's perfect lover and beloved".[26]

As this is only a sample of the available interpretations of Piers, it will be helpful if I state my own working hypothesis for understanding his figural role. The hypothesis will be tested as I take particular passages from the poem, and can be adjusted if the demands of the poetry and its images in a particular context make adjustment

---

[17] Bloomfield, Piers Plowman (New Brunswick, 1961), see 107 (149), 134: Bloomfield also thinks Piers "turns out to be the human aspect of Christ", "the ideal Pope", and that he is even "deified", essay reprinted in Interpretations of Piers Plowman, ed. E. Vasta (Notre Dame, 1968), 342, 343, 346.

[18] F. Carnegy, The Relations between the Social and Divine Order in . . . Piers the Plowman (Breslau, 1934), 39, 47.

[19] Donaldson, Piers Plowman, 163, 179, 184.

[20] Lucidly argued by Dunning, "The Structure of the B-Test of Piers Plowman", reprinted in Interpretations of Piers Plowman, ed. Vasta, 259–77, especially see 268–9.

[21] Dunning, Piers Plowman (London, 1937), 138; Frank, Piers Plowman, see 81, 33, 23.

[22] G. K. Patch, "The Allegorical Characters in Piers Plowman", unpublished dissertation (Stanford University, 1957).

[23] Robertson and Huppé, Piers Plowman, 6–7.

[24] A. H. Smith, Piers Plowman (London, 1951), 1.

[25] H. W. Troyer, "Who is Piers Plowman?" PMLA, 47 (1932), 368–84, see 373, 376–7.

[26] E. Vasta, The Spiritual Basis of Piers Plowman (The Hague, 1965), 132–35.

necessary—we must of course guard against the danger of violating the poem to make its symbols produce a reading predetermined and fixed by the critic.

St Paul writes in 1 Corinthians 9.22, "I became all things to all men that I might save all", and this paraphrases the centre of my hypothesis about Piers's function in the poem. Piers has undeniably been all things to all critics, and in the poem itself he sets up reactions ranging from reverential association with Christ (XV.206) to Waster's —he "sette Pieres at a pees and his plow bothe" (VI.171). By Passus XV the dreamer has become convinced that Piers has some saving powers. He sees Piers differently at different stages of his pilgrimage and so do we. For as we follow the dreams through the eyes and words of the dreamer-poet-pilgrim our perspective tends to merge into his. How we see things is at least in part a reflection of our own situation and mental state:

If Perceptive Organs vary: Objects of Perception seem to vary:
If the Perceptive Organs close: their objects seem to close also:

Blake is here developing an ancient principle, putting it to his own use.[27] Earlier, for example, pseudo-Dionysius had argued that perception is "corresponding to each separate creature's powers", and if man fails to see God it is as if a man should fail to see the sun: "this is not due to any weakness or deficiency in its distribution of the light, but is due to the unreceptiveness of those creatures which do not attain sufficient singleness to participate therein." Just so, the devils retain their angelic gifts but "themselves do not perceive it through blinding of their faculties of spiritual perception".[28] It is no surprise to find so basic and common a notion running through fourteenth-century vernacular works such as *The Cloud of unknowing* and Julian of Norwich's *Revelations of Divine Love*.[29] In fact, it was once briefly associated with Piers by E. Vasta: "the way Piers is seen and understood is determined by the degree of spiritual progress reached by other souls." But unfortunately, at least from my point of view, Vasta also states[30] that we should understand

---

[27] *Jerusalem*, 30 [34]; of course, Blake has a radical understanding of the way social existence and labour affects perception (e.g. *Jerusalem*, 65.12–28), and one can't claim any such insight for Langland. For examples of the tradition preceding Langland: Daniel 10.7; Luke 24.31; Plato, *Phaedrus*, 250–1; Plotinus, *Enneads*, I.6.6; I.6.7; II.9.2; VI.5.12, etc: Boethius, *Consolation of Philosophy*, V pr. 4; V m. 4; V pr. 6.

[28] *On the Divine Names and The Mystical Theology*, ed. and trans. C. E. Rolt (reprint London, 1966), 54, 92, 122; similarly Augustine, *City of God* XXII.29.

[29] *The Cloud of Unknowing*, EETS, 218 (1944), for example chapters 4, 6, 14–26, 68; Julian of Norwich, *Revelations of Divine Love*, ed. G. Warwick (13th, reprinted London, 1958), e.g., pages 22, 24, 26, 53, 55–6, etc.

[30] Vasta, *The Spiritual Basis of Piers Plowman*, 132, 134, 137, 138.

Piers's function as "equivalent" to the Bride's in the Canticle, that "Piers is ideal earthly perfection . . . perfect from first to his last; he does not grow in spiritual perfection with each of his appearances nor undergo a change in his spiritual condition." He goes on to speak of "the deified Piers". However, I do not think the figure of Piers in Passus V-VI is identical to Piers in Passus XVI or XIX, and he seems to me a figure with rather less independent existence than Vasta's Piers, more the "objective correlative" of the perceiving mind than Vasta's perfect and unchanging Piers. I do not believe we should assume that "Piers is ideal earthly perfection" or that "he is perfect from first to his last". In the hypothesis offered here he is less consistently "out there" than Vasta's comments imply; he is much more a focal point for a range of perceptions and notions seen through the characters' visions. In so far as he *is* "out there", we can think of his actions in the capacity suggested by the quotation from Paul's letter to the Corinthians: he becomes to the perceivers the means by which they hope to be guided to salvation, and the particular qualities Piers figures and embodies at any point are indissolubly linked to the knower's mode of perception at that stage, in that context. This outlines my working hypothesis for the figure Piers. He appears and acts towards all men as the saving agent appropriate to their own perception, tending to embody what Langland takes to be the best insights available at particular stages and contexts in the poem. In this way he also shows us the stage dreamer and reader have reached in the poem's search. It should also be noted that the hypothesis does allow for the possibility of dreamer and reader reaching a different, perhaps deeper, awareness than other characters within the poem and so seeing Piers differently to them.

We will now plunge into the deep end by studying the complex and controversial passage which centres on the tree of Charity (B XVI). This is a suitable place for exploring Langland's treatment of images, ideas and temporal dimensions. But first I will examine the way critics have elucidated this part of *Piers Plowman*: not only will this provide us with the current interpretations of an extremely concentrated piece of writing, it also allows us to scrutinize current critical methods for reading allegorical poetry.

In his book on *Piers Plowman* Donaldson carried out a thorough study of the tree of Charity and its C-text parallel (C XIX). The conclusions of such a distinguished medievalist must carry weight, and his analysis of the B-text passage in question should be worth summarizing. He finds "a pluralizing of the tree image that threatens to turn the garden into a forest" (188)—even the way the tree's fruit "represent the conditions of human life" is unprepared for (183-4). Thinking about the temporal dimensions of the passage, he correctly and convincingly raised "several serious obstacles" to the view that the passage is "a single allegory dealing with the pre-Christian era'

(186–7). Nevertheless he concludes, "I believe, however, that one can read it as a pre-Christian allegory without encountering too many inconsistencies" (188). Discussing Piers he finds the "division of labour between Piers and free will" quite unintelligible, but this is the least of the troubles here (187). Donaldson claims that in B XV we were offered an "identification" of Piers with Christ, and that we are therefore "fully prepared" in B XVI, "to recognize him as Christ" (182, 183); however, B XVI. 36–7 causes "some awkwardness ... if he stands for Christ", and his felling of the fruit "also seems strange if he is indeed the saviour" (184). When Piers uses the second prop, "he could not very well represent the human nature of Christ, since Christ had not yet assumed human nature, although he could represent the human nature which Christ was to assume, or ... the second person of the Trinity before the Incarnation." However, around XVI.93, "one might argue ... that Piers stands for God the Father" (184). Donaldson suggests that in Passus XV there is a "Christ-Piers identification", but he then finds that it "does not fit the vision of the Tree of Charity": from this position he finds it "extremely attractive" to insist with Burdach that Piers is never identified with Christ but is always "a man", and one who is associated with St Peter: "[Piers] is mankind, or rather that elevated portion of mankind which includes the patriarchs and prophets ... and others who prefigured Christ before the Incarnation" (185–6). Despite this, once he gets angry he "becomes the human nature of Christ, the Son of Mary", although one "is always recognizing in him ... the simple farmer" (186–7, 188).

This summary conveys the critic's almost desperate amassing of propositions which might be extracted from the symbolic figure of Piers and the surrounding images. The approach inevitably leads him to conclude with a fairly comprehensive statement about Langland's ineptitude and failure to articulate his ideas in the tree of Charity passage: "The allegory seems too complex, too crowded ... One can only conclude that in his composition B got hold of an idea of such poetic splendor that he became blinded to its remoter ramifications and particularly to its extension into the field of logic." On top of this, "Piers remains ambiguous and even redundant" (187). But among the questions which arise from this critique are whether Donaldson and Langland have the same approach to allegorical imagery and its "logic", whether the critic's conclusions about the nature of Langland's models are justified, whether he or the poet is confused or whether they are both confused. These questions will be met by carrying out our own analysis of the passage and at the moment it is sufficient to notice how Donaldson seems to assume that Langland is using the kind of picture models that dominated medieval figurative practice—for example, "Piers stands for God the Father"; along with this goes the assumption that Piers is the kind of model from which we ought to be able to read off some second terms from theological dogmatics. Donaldson's critique is worth recalling at such length because he is a medievalist particularly concerned with the text of a poem rather than with exegetical "sources".

R. W. Frank's work is also at the opposite pole to Robertson's, yet he too becomes extremely irritated with Langland. He agrees with Bloomfield that the tree of Charity belongs to the *Lignum Vitae* genre, and he agrees with Burdach and Donaldson that the tree passage "is a 'single allegory dealing with the pre-Christian era'". From this perspective he takes the inner vision of B XVI as "a mechanical repetition of a novel device, whose probable purpose...is to present in narrative form the fact that man could not be saved without certain gifts from Christ dramatized in later passus of *Dobet*". It seems to him that there is "confusion" in this inner vision, and here he mostly follows Donaldson. He does, however, offer an explanation for it. Langland was apparently unable "to say two things at the same time"; these two things Frank finds he himself can express easily: "that man has free will, is free to sin or not to sin, and that man is assisted in the fight against sin by the Three Persons of the Trinity". In Langland's poetry, Frank complains, "free will is associated only with grace and the Holy Ghost." Worse still, "the logic of the image" is broken because the third person of the Trinity does not fight the third aggressor, "but fights only when the world, the flesh, and the devil combine to attack man". The root of the "confusion" is that "the poet has not solved the problem of expressing simultaneously two ideas, that man has free will and that he is assisted by the Trinity."[31] But Langland would have had no difficulty in producing the kind of picture model Frank is demanding. He could have shown a figure beating off attackers and using three necessary props to do so. Then he could have read off, "free will", "assisted by the Trinity"— "simultaneously"—beats off the devil and his confederates. I doubt that Langland was at this point trying to write the kind of model Frank envisages, or that he is incapable of expressing rather more than two complex ideas simultaneously. My own analysis will attempt to illustrate this.

Once more the critic's assumptions about allegorical imagery are revealing. We have seen that he thinks Langland's "type" of allegory ("personification-allegory") asks the reader to "make at most *one* translation to understand the allegory", while "symbol-allegory" calls for "two translations". This may perhaps be good advice for reading many of the figures we have met so far (chapters two and three). But Frank attempts to apply it to Passus XVI. He tells us, "this is the meaning of the scene in which the devil carries

---

[31] Frank, *Piers Plowman*, see 86, notes 8–9, 87.

off to hell the fruit (the souls of the just)": "With the help of the Trinity, man can do good deeds. But man's good deeds alone will not win salvation." The scene is followed by "the announcement that the souls of the just will be rescued and with a summary narrative of Jesus' life up to the moment of his imprisonment". This sounds simple enough, and we are surprised Langland should have made such an elaborate mess of conveying so basic a dogmatic point— although it is more "paradoxical" than Frank assumes. Not only would we have to admit with Donaldson that Piers is "redundant" but that much else is also merely irrelevant, or obscure for obscurity's sake. But actually Frank is reading *Piers Plowman*, in his own words, "as a literal rather than an allegorical poem". So when he meets this extended "metaphor" he simply carries out a "decortexing" operation worthy of any medieval exegete or modern Robertsonian.[32] From what he takes to be a cryptographic picturing model he has neatly read off his version of the dogmatic propositions he thinks the poet was trying to assert. Or, looking at it from another angle, he has substituted his idea of the doctrinal complex for the poet's idea which takes form in that particular complex structure of words. To Frank, the "meaning" of the passage is better put without the poet's idiosyncratic obfuscation, and so he makes his "translation" for us.[33]

Turning to Robertson and Huppé we see the usual imitation of exegetical norms. The tree is "the tree of Charity, the *lignum vitae* of Scripture, [and] represents Christ or the Cross anagogically [*sic*], the just allegorically, and the individual tropologically".[34] It is also "the life of Christ on earth", while its fruit symbolize "salvation"— because Bruno reads the fruit of the tree of Life in the Apocalypse as the fruit of salvation.[35] When Piers knocks the fruit down the scholars comment, "That is, he knocks down the allegorical fruits which grew on the tree before Christ brought charity to the world, the just men of the Old Testament." It is interesting that these critics observe no shift of allegorical mode from the outer dream to the inner vision. They extract doctrinal propositions from any stage of the poet's writing without attempting to discriminate between different kinds of model. I have already discussed their characteristic methodology and it is employed here. Assuming that Langland's

---

[32] Frank, "The Art of Reading Medieval Personification-Allegory", *ELH*, (1953), 237–50, reprinted in *Interpretations of Piers Plowman*, ed. Vasta, 225, and Frank, *Piers Plowman*, 85–6.

[33] On Frank's side, M. W. Bloomfield, "Symbolism in Medieval Literature", *M Phil*, 56 (1958), 73–81; later article, "A Grammatical Approach to Personification-Allegory", *M Phil*, 60 (1962–3), 161–71.

[34] *Piers Plowman*, 191 (even these exegetical specialists slip up here over the anagogic sense—see note 15 above).

[35] *Piers Plowman*, 192 n. 35; the next quotation is from 196.

tree at once takes us to a specific Biblical text they introduce Apocalypse 22.2: "the tree of Life [*lignum vitae*], bearing twelve fruits,
yielding its fruits every month: and the leaves of the tree were for the
healing of the nations". Naturally enough, the exegetical tradition
understood the fruit of this tree as the fruit of eternal life, salvation.
But it is not at all clear that the fruit of a tree called Patience or
Charity is necessarily equivalent to the *lignum vitae* of Apocalypse
22.2. And if the trees are not equivalent, then Robertson and
Huppé's importing of Apocalypse 22 and its exegetical tradition to
elucidate Langland's tree, grown in a separate garden, will seem a
piece of eccentric irrelevancy. It should cause some surprise that if
the trees are equivalent, Langland failed to remember that his own
tree's leaves should be "for the healing of the nations", or that the
tree's fruit should be "bearing twelve fruits, yielding its fruits every
month", and failed to suggest that his fruit actually does offer or
represent eternal salvation. Once again my own analysis will impli-
citly challenge these critics, confronting the assumption they share
with Donaldson and Frank—that Langland was trying to write
picture models throughout this section, and that he intended us to
read his poem accordingly.

We found Ben Smith among the scholars who approve of Robertson and Huppé's critical methods, and he himself has written a
chapter on the tree of Charity in which he states that the reader's
imagination is "largely controlled", not by the poet's contexts but
"by the traditional association of the figure".[36] He claims that the
tree reflects "the tree of Jesse", "the tree of Life", "the tree of the
Cross", "the tree of the descent of mankind from Adam", "the
tree of virtues" and "the tree of wisdom".[37] Although many of these
interpretations will be challenged below we may as well point out
now that a Jesse tree without the Virgin Mary, without Jesse and
without Christ is not a Jesse tree.[38] Furthermore, Smith's claim that
Langland's tree represents the Cross fails to establish any definite
connection between the tree in Passus XVI and the text of Ephesians
3.16–19: in fact, his procedure in importing the traditional exegesis
of Ephensians 3.16–19 to illuminate Langland's tree involves a
classic example of Robertsonian methodology. First he asserts that
Anima's tree reflects the *lignum vitae* of Genesis 2.9: this is maintained
although Anima's own exegesis does not coincide with Smith's. Then
he correctly remarks that the *lignum vitae* of Genesis was traditionally
associated with the *lignum crucis*. But, Smith carries on, Ephesians

---

[36] Smith, *Traditional Imagery of Charity in Piers Plowman*, 59.
[37] *ibid.*, respectively, 59, 61–4; 59, 63–7; 59, 71–2; 66.
[38] Even the extension of the Jesse tree back to Adam is rare—see E. Watson,
Early Iconography of the Tree of Jesse (London, 1934) and A. Katzenellenbogen,
Allegories of the Virtues and Vices in Medieval Art (London, 1939), 52 ff.

3.16–19 was also associated with the tree of Life and the Cross, as the Lombard's commentary on St Paul witnesses. In this commentary the exegete "equates *latitudo* with the transverse member of the Cross, which, he says, pertains to good works". Following this kind of exegesis all four pieces of the cross are drawn out of St Paul's words on the breadth, length, depth and height of love which he prays will strengthen the Ephesians; having done this, the exegete reads off appropriate ethical sentiments for each member. This exegesis, Smith maintains, has "far-reaching implications for Langland's description of the tree of Charity". Here are the implications: Lombard equated *longitudo* of Ephesians 3.18 with the upright of the Cross; and the upright of the Cross signifies "perseverentiam"; but, says Smith, "a relationship or approximate equation exists between *perseverentia* and M[iddle] E[nglish] *pacience;*" and Langland's tree is called "Pacience" (XVI.8). Therefore Langland's line (XVI.8) "depends upon a conventional connection between the main longitudinal section of the tree of the Cross and *perseverentiam*".[39] Ben Smith's manoeuvres are not only completely extra-literary but they are also circular. His leap to Lombard on Ephesians 3.16–19 depends on already having assumed that Langland's tree in Passus XVI signifies the life-giving tree of the Cross, and that the upright of Langland's tree is more important than the fact that it has no transversals. The scholar's procedure also ignores the extremely explicit nature of Anima's exegesis and the significance this might have. It is unlikely that such an exegete as Anima would have failed to label the members of the Cross in her model. Ben Smith, like the other medievalists just considered, assumes that Langland's images and modes are all of a piece, that piece comprising a series of picture models as employed by exegetes and preachers. His confident equating of exegetes and Langland is based on this assumption.

These are the main efforts that have been made to elucidate Langland's complex imagery around the tree in Passus XVI.[40] In most readings of the passage there is a striking failure to remain aware of the poet's own imagistic process, an unquestioning readiness either to substitute exegetes' interpretations of other images in other contexts for Langland's own images, or to suppose that Langland wished to convey a series of easily stated propositions hidden in an obscuring metaphoric overcoat. The possibility that the

---

[39] *Traditional Imagery of Charity in Piers Plowman*, 64–6 *passim*.
[40] Another line of argument which I shall confront briefly below is that, "Piers shaking the fruit from the tree is itself an obvious allegory of the fall of man" and demands interpretation by the exegetical senses: Kaske *JEGP*, 62 (1963), 202 ff.; see too Fowler, *Piers Plowman*, chapter four; Mills, "The Role of the Dreamer in *Piers Plowman*", in *Piers Plowman: Critical Approaches*, ed. S. S. Hussey (London, 1969), 202; Kirk, *Dream Thought of Piers Plowman*, 159, 168–70, 182, 190.

poet is deploying different modes of figurative expression within an organic poetic process does not seem to have been given much attention. Nevertheless, I shall argue that Langland's poetry embodies such a process.

The controversial passage is launched by the dreamer's continued bafflement about the nature of Charity:

> Ac ȝet I am in a were what charite is to mene
>
> (XVI.3)

Near the beginning of the previous passus the dreamer had asked: "What is Charite?" (XV.145). He received an answer resting on Matthew 18.8 and the generosity native to Charity. But he is un-satisfied and questions Anima: "Where shoulde men fynde such a frende with so fre an herte?" (XV.147) He admits he has never met such a person and this leads him into the striking image we discussed in the last chapter:

> Clerkis kenne me that Cryst is in alle places;
> Ac I seygh hym neuere sothly but as my-self in a miroure,
> *Ita in enigmate, tunc facie ad faciem*
>
> (XV.156–7)

Thus the dreamer, Will, vaguely associates Charity both with Christ and with his own introspection. The nearest he has come to seeing Charity, or Christ, is by going into his own soul, that is by intro-spection. This idea depends on the notion that the Soul is made in the image of God (Genesis 1.26), a notion classically developed by St Augustine in his *De Trinitate*. In Augustine's view it is by the image of God in man's soul that the mind becomes able and powerful to cleave to God whose image it is. Self-understanding thus has a special and necessary role in spiritual development.[41] But Anima also assures Will that "with-outen helpe of Piers Plowman ... his persone seestow neuere" (XV.190). This is because Piers has a godlike inwardness with the individual will (XV.193–4). Soon after-wards Anima makes the famous association of Piers and Christ. The dreamer, Anima says, can only know Charity, "thorw will one". But this insight is open to "No clerke ne creature", but only to "Piers the Plowman, *Petrus, id est, Christus*" (XV.205–6). The dreamer is not going to be able to "fynde" Charity without both introspection and the "helpe of Piers Plowman". Now this help from Piers Plowman will be in a form in which Piers can be associated with Christ: "*Petrus, id est, Christus*". Many critics have written many

---

[41] XII.7.9–10; XII.11.16; XIV.14.20; XV.7.11.

words about this conjunction and our previous account of interpretations of the Piers figure showed how he has been identified with
Christ in various ways. Donaldson, in his work on the tree passage,
claims that the line linking Piers and Christ (XV.206) prepares us to
recognize Piers as Christ in the next passus. But any attempt to
reduce Langland's mode here to the kind which makes us say that
Piers "stands for Christ" (Donaldson), is disastrous. It is important
to make this clear before proceeding, because the lines from B XV
which we have so far quoted are closely related to the tree of Charity.
If we mishandle Langland's writing at this point, we are going to do
so in Passus XVI.

We have met the exegetes' "id est" frequently in earlier
chapters as time and again it was used in figurative picturing models.
Now R. E. Kaske has claimed that in XV.203–6 Langland is using,
"a recognizable cliché of biblical exegesis". But we should note the
mode this leads Kaske to assume:

> *Petrus* (the Apostle and through him the prelacy) *stands for Christ* in
> the visible history of the Church Militant, just as *petra* (the rock)
> "stands for Christ" in the text of Scripture. (Mtt.16.18) . . .

> Langland is extending Christ's own pun on *Petrus* and *petra* to
> embrace also the great exegetical commonplace of Christ Himself
> as *petra*, an extension already familiar in commentaries on the
> verse.[42] [His italics]

Inevitably we are back to the very models of the exegetes, and
Langland is only doing what is "already familiar in commentaries on
the verse" (Mtt.16.18). Before seeing whether this is all there is to be
said on the matter, I will give some more examples of the exegetes'
and homilists' use of the "id est" technique when relating Christ to
a first term. We will then be able to judge how relevant they are to
Langland's "id est".

In his twenty-fourth lecture on the Book of Wisdom the fourteenth-century Dominican, Robert Holcot, relates Ovid's account of
Hercules strangling the two snakes which Juno, Jove's wife, sent to
kill him. The whole is read in a way we are by now familiar with—
as a picturing model, and with all the limitations of the naive variety.
The piece that concerns us at the moment, however, is the gloss on
the fact that Hercules killed the snakes (read as "Angues tentationis")
and so showed himself: "the son of Jove: that is of Christ [filium

---

[42] In *Critical Approaches to Medieval Literature*, ed. D. Bethurum (New York,
1960), 40–1; also Kirk, *Dream Thought of Piers Plowman*, 163–4.

Jovis: id est Christi]".[43] Here then, Ovid's Jove is connected with
Christ by an "id est". Still in the late Middle Ages, a collection of
sermons we have already used contains two relevant statements in
different sermons:

> Apollo, þat is . . . Crist, Goddes sone of heuene. . . .
> Codrus, þat is vr blessid sauiur Crist Iesu.[44]

Here the exegetes' "id est" appears in English as "þat is", joining
Christ and another term. Similarly Rabanus, commenting on the
Book of Ruth says that Booz "is our redeemer [est redeptor
noster]".[45] Although the use of "id est" doubtless encouraged the
exegetes to turn the events and images into picture models, the links
being made should not have necessitated such an outcome. For
example, when Mirk comments, " Moyses, þe which was a figur of our
Lord Ihesu Crist", he could as easily have used "id est" as "figur
of" (though he would probably have then been tempted to develop a
picture model); the *rationale* is the same in both cases.[46] I have frequently argued that we must not short-circuit the task of concrete
analysis by simply pointing to the writer's choice of terms or definitions, and that the same mode can hide under a variety of terms and
definitions: it should be possible to use "id est" without developing
naive picture models just as Mirk, on this occasion, uses "figur of"
without developing his habitual modes.

Langland's "*Petrus, id est, Christus*" does not seem to me the kind
of figure Kaske claims ("*Petrus . . . stands for Christ*"), nor does it
seem to be "an extension already familiar in commentaries" on
Matthew 16.18. It seems far more accurate to say that Langland
avoids the models employed by commentaries, which we examined
in chapters two and three. The poet develops his own context around
a doubtful dreamer who has just shown an awareness that Charity is
to be found somehow associated with Christ, and somehow, *in
enigmate*, through introspection. It is in *this* context that Anima's
emphasis on the need for the "helpe of Piers Plowman" if the vision
of Charity is to be achieved, is followed by the conjunction "*Petrus,
id est, Christus*". There is no picture model here, no definitive
"identification" of Piers with Christ, no cause for us to expect that
in Passus XVI we must be ready "to recognize him as Christ", no
cause for us to mimic medieval exegetes and assume we are to read off
a series of formulated propositions from Piers whenever he enters the

---

[43] *In Librum Sapentiae Salomonis Praelectioners* CCXIII (Basle, 1586), *lectio* XXIV,
86–7.
[44] *Three Middle English Sermons*, ed. D. M. Grisdale (Kendal, 1939), 13, 68.
[45] *P. Lat.* 108. 1205.
[46] *Festial*, EETS, 96 (1905), 101.

poem. What Anima has done is to complete the fusion of the dreamer's probings at this point with her own emphasis that the dreamer (and reader) cannot see Charity without Piers's help. But where Piers is both the way and the focus for such an insight—an insight to the very "persone" of Charity—he will surely be in very close relation to that which he discloses.[47] And that which he discloses is Charity; but the dreamer, as we showed, has himself dimly realized that the "persone" of Charity and Christ are themselves in very close relationship. Anima is confirming that Piers is to be the lens through which Charity's "persone" is finally disclosed to him. Thus, for his purposes, and at this stage of his spiritual journey, he may be told "Petrus, id est, Christus". This is preparation for the disclosures to be created from Passus XVI onwards, disclosures involving Will, Piers, Charity and Christ. In the terms of my working hypothesis for Piers, we might expect "Petrus, id est, Christus" to suggest that when the dreamer's spiritual perception, for which Piers is the symbol and the lens, attains the vision of Charity's "persone", and so of Christ, then in some way there will appear to be a merging of the symbol and lens of his spiritual perception with the disclosed Christ-Charity. In what form the disclosure will be made we could not possibly anticipate at this point. But let us not impatiently turn the kind of process Langland seems to be creating, into that of the exegetes, homilists and normal medieval allegorical poets.

This is the background of the dreamer's question at the opening of Passus XVI. However, another earlier context is also relevant. In BXIII Clergye had found himself unable to explain precisely the nature of Dowel. But he knew that Piers Plowman "settle all sciences at a soppe saue love one". Conscience admits the difficulty of such attempted definitions ("I can nouȝt her-on"), but comments:

> ac I knowe wel Pieres
>
> . . .
>
> Thanne passe we ouer til Piers come and preue this in dede.
>
> (XIII.130; 132: see 118-32)

So there too Piers was seen both in conjunction with Charity and as the resolving lens. He is the one Conscience knows, and Conscience trusts that he will, at some stage, enact a resolution of the enigmas.

We are now, at last, coming to that stage. Will's question, "What charite is to mene" (XVI.3), leads to Anima's allegorical tree. We must remember that Anima made it plain in Passus XV that it is only

---

[47] Compare Coleridge on symbolism in The Stateman's Manual, Lay Sermons, ed. R. J. White (London, 1972), 28–31, and the heading to chapter four, above, from Notebooks, II.2274.

through Piers that we will encounter Charity's "persone". She her-self will not suffice, despite her hints and helpings in that passus. If we do remember this we may better appreciate and recognize Langland's discriminations between the uses of different allegorical modes in the passages under discussion.[48] Anima's tree is offered as a picture model of the kind so familiar to students of medieval writing (Elizabeth Salter has appropriately likened it to "a diagram"[49]). 1 Corinthians 13.4 states that "Charity is patient", and Anima de-picts this in her "diagram", calling the tree both "Charite" and "Pacience": tree = patience = charity (XVI.3–4; 8). She is trying to convey how "groweth the frute Charite", and the only mode she uses attempts to freeze the process of growth into a timeless scale model, to fix its parts into neatly and definitively formulated labels. The parts of the growth of Charity are read off the model with a confidence and rigour worthy of an exegete:

> Mercy is the more ther-of the myddel stoke is Reuthe.
> The leues ben Lele-Wordes the lawe of Holy cherche

and so on (XVI.4–17). There is no justification for critics to read off more information from this allegorical scale model than the inter-preter Anima does. Had Anima (our exegete at this stage) wished to convey information about the tree of the Cross, the tree of Life, or about the longitudinal member of the Cross, above ground signifying *perseverentia*, she would have done so in the mode she has decided to use. And the chosen model cannot on its own suggest these additional readings (Ben Smith's), for it is a limited model of narrowly limited purposes. It would doubtless have satisfied most medieval figural writers, such as Usk, who in his *Testament of Love* defines the growth of the fruit of salvation from such a tree model.[50] But the definitive-ness of the mode, its very facility, is specious; it can suggest no resolutions to the problems involved in thinking about the growth of Charity, through *Liberum Arbitrium*, "thorw god and thorw good men", nor can it disclose to us, "what charite is to mene". It fails to disclose the second term readings. And Langland, being neither Usk, nor medieval homilist, nor medieval exegete, did not think it resolved the dreamer's queries. The cue for a deeper inquiry into the nature of the *growth* of Charity comes in Anima's last line. Man's *Liberum Arbitrium* has to "ferme" man's garden ("herte"), which God himself made. But Man's "Free Judgement" is not immediately under God, but set, "Vnder Piers the Plowman to pyken it and to

---

[48] See Elizabeth Salter, *Piers Plowman*, 73–6.
[49] *ibid.*, 74; compare the trees in MS. Ad 37409, British Museum.
[50] *Testament of Love*, II.7, while III.4–7 is also relevant.

weden it" (XVI.17). Given our analysis of the relevant passages in Passus XV and XVI, the dreamer's ecstatic reaction on hearing the name "Piers the Plowman" will not seem unmotivated (but nor will it demand Donaldson's reading): the reader will be as expectant as the dreamer. Unlike Ben Smith and his colleagues (typical medieval exegetes), but like William Langland, we will not read off most of the answers for which the poet is searching, from Anima's attempted scale-model.

Langland's dreamer does not at once focus on the figure of Piers Plowman. He "swouned",

> And laye longe in a lone dreme and atte laste me thouʒte,
> That Pieres the Plowman al the place me shewed,
> And bad me toten on the tree on toppe and on rote.
> (XVI.20–22)

Through this protracted "lone dreme", Will, "atte laste", becomes collected enough to think of Piers Plowman, and to see this figure in his swoon. The "place" Anima described remains in his memory. I mention this because we should recall that Anima's model was a descriptive sketch—Will was not *shown* anything. It is through Piers that Anima's allegorical description is turned to visionary "shewynge" (see BXVI.1). Piers' order to "toten on the tree" is an order to re-examine our received model and information.

Now the dreamer sees that the tree is underpropped by three "piles". In explaining their function Piers uses Psalm 36.24: "*Cum ceciderit iustus non collidetur: quia Dominus supponit manum suam*" (XVI.25). This is a Psalm of trust and patience (vv.1, 3, 7) and the verse Langland quotes is one of the verses of promise. Though the just fall, "he shall not be utterly cast down [non collidetur]". The promise is that these holy men ("sanctos suos", v.28) shall inherit the land, since God will not leave the just in the hands of the wicked (vv.29, 33). The Psalm makes it plain that the just can and do gain mercy, patience and goodness, but that nevertheless their final salvation depends completely on God; in the words of the verse Langland quotes, "quia Dominus supponit manum suam".[51] The full implications of Langland's choice of this verse will become clear later, but we must be aware of at least these nuances at this stage. We will see that "the just" must indeed fall.

But for the moment the dreamer is being shown how the props support the tree. This brings us to one of the sections Donaldson found unintelligible. Here we must study the kind of relationship that

---

[51] One of the qualities of the Just in the Psalm is Mercy (v.21), and this is the root of Anima's tree of Charity.

may exist between the tree Anima used and the way Piers develops it. The possibilities can be exemplified by concentrating on XVI.30–35. This passage is chosen because Elizabeth Salter has interestingly used these lines to dissociate totally Anima's exegesis from Piers's explanations, and because this recalls Donaldson's complaint about such "a pluralizing of the tree image, that the garden threatens to become a forest".[52] Elizabeth Salter writes on XVI.30–35:

> If we interpret this strictly the meaning is curious: the temptations of the flesh are levelled against obedient speech and kind looks— all that is left after they have done their work, is the bare text of God's Scriptures. This is, of course, based upon a forced, out of context reading of the second passage.[53]

Now I have already noted her contention that Langland's allegory involves "many different modes", and acknowledged that this is basic to any relevant approach to *Piers Plowman's* figures. And certainly we do not wish to act like some modern critics or medieval exegetes, disregarding differences of modes and contexts. Nonetheless it *may* be that Anima's parabolic and stereotyped exegesis actually grows into the second image and is given a resonance it formerly lacked. Piers states that the lust of the flesh (compare XI.11 ff.) acts as a "fel wynde" which "norissheth nice siꝫtes" and also "wordes/and wikked werkes ther-of wermes of synne". The result of this carnality is that the blossoms are bitten "riꝫt to the bare leues". Elizabeth Salter has shown how Anima's exegesis would interpret the allegory here and its "curious" result. But let us suppose that the poet or dreamer has not simply forgotten Anima's gloss: "The leues ben Lele-Wordes the lawe of Holycherche" (XVI.6). Now the effects of the wind of Carnality include not only the destruction of all possibility of fruition, but also the reduction of the plant "to the bare leues", which, as Professor Salter says, would suggest to Anima's reader, "the bare text of God's Scripture". But in the new context this gloss has striking ramifications. For Carnality, in medieval thought, causes "the death of the soul"; and one of its manifestations is when the text of God's Scripture is reduced to a barely literal understanding.[54] In Passus X Scripture told the dreamer that although Saracens and Jews may be saved simply by Baptism, the case is different for Christians. This is because Christ "conformed the lawe" for Christians in a new way; salvation became conditional on love:

---

[52] I summarized Donaldson's handling of the tree earlier: see *Piers Plowman*, 188.
[53] Salter, *Piers Plowman*, 75.
[54] For example, Augustine, *City of God*, III.14 and see Robertson, *Preface*, 272.

Si cum Christo surrexistis, etc.,
He shulde louye and leue and the law fulfille.
That is—"loue thi lorde god leuest aboue alle,
And after, alle Crystene creatures in commune, eche man other;"

(X.355–8)

Christ's acts fulfilled the letter of the Old Law and turned the law
from an external one of the letter to an internal, "spiritual" one
which can only be fulfilled by faith and charity. Christ "confermed
the lawe" by revealing it fulfilled and transformed in charity.[55] The
old law, the bare letter, now becames a letter which kills (2 Cor. 3.6;
Rom. 3.20; Rom 7.6). And in passus XVI the first and limited
writer-exegete stated that besides being "Lele-wordes" the leaves
are "the *lawe* of Holycherche" (XVI.6 my italics). So if we keep
Anima's gloss in mind as Piers develops the new context, it may be
hinted that the wind of Carnality not only deflowers the tree of
Charity, so preventing spiritual fruition, but also debars man from
the saving love evidenced in Christ's sacrifice, a sacrifice which
delivered man from subjection to the bare law. This wind again
subjects man to the bare law and its letter, and this can kill the soul.
Perhaps in this way the poet *may* be alluding to Anima's earlier
mechanistic gloss, but now invoking the weight of Pauline ideas about
the law of the letter, and the living spirit, to suggest the final effects
of the wind of Carnality. Anima's easy formulation is placed into an
active and challenging context, within a piece of allegorical writing
which is itself modally very different.

Another problem which has puzzled and irritated some scholars
is Langland's time-scheme. The passage we have just considered
leads us into this problem, although we shall return to it again. One
of the distinguishing marks of much of Langland's allegorical
writing is his handling of temporal dimensions, which is, I believe,
both poetically and theologically dazzling.

Piers tells the dreamer that against the carnal wind,

     sette I the secounde pile *sapiencia-Dei-patris*,
  That is, the passioun and the powre of owre prynce Iesu,
  Thorw preyeres and thorw penaunces and goddes passioun in
     mynde,
  I saue it til I se it rypen and somdel y-fruited.

(XVI.36–9)

First it should be noted that these lines confute the attempts of
critics to generalize the whole allegory into the "pre-Christian"

---

[55] See Matthew 5.17.

era.[56] Piers, acting as Will's exegete, uses the English for "id est" to keep him aware that the props function metaphorically. And as St Thomas explained that when sacred writers referred to "the arm of God" they figure God's power of doing and making ("virtus operativa"), so when Piers speaks of seizing the second prop, *sapiencia-Dei-patris*, we are to realize that in some way Piers is making use of the operative power of the Son.[57] Piers himself acknowledges this when he explains his use of the second prop: "that is, the passioun and the powre of owre prynce Iesu". (The choice of the name "Iesu" is precise, for this emphasises that the power is made available by the *Incarnate* Wisdom—"Iesu" being His name on earth.) At this point then, the fourteenth-century dreamer is involved in a vision whose content is clearly post-Resurrection.

Secondly we must try to understand the relationship the poet suggests between the dreamer's Piers, at this moment, and "owre prynce Iesu". Here Will has not yet been able to focus his vision on Christ directly. The nearest he came to this was the record in Passus XV of his own introspection which led him to an enigmatic view of Christ-charity. By the beginning of Passus XVIII he will be ready to dream "of Crystes passioun and penaunce the peple that of-rauȝte" (XVIII.6). But now (XVI) he depends on the figure Piers to tell him about the effects of prayer, penance, "and goddes passioun in mynde" (XVI.38). These effects, Piers says, save the tree "til I se it rypen and somdel y-fruited". Again the fruit and tree of Anima's "diagram" are being absorbed into a richer context. But, we may wonder, in what way can Piers be seen to wield "the powre of owre prynce Iesu", to bring "goddes passioun in mynde" and so aid the spiritual growth with which the poet is concerned? Answering this inquiry will provide a good example of one of the ways this poet uses allegory as a *process*. In Passus XIX Conscience tells the dreamer that after his resurrection Christ "ȝaf Pieres power" (XIX.178), and later in that Passus, advising men to partake of the Sacramental food he says:

> Grace thorw goddes worde gaue Pieres power,
> And myȝtes to maken it and men to ete it after,
> In helpe of her hele . . .
>
> (XIX.384–6)

So by the stage of the vision depicted in these quotations from Passus XIX Piers has become a focal figure for the dreamer's understanding of the mysterious communication of the "power" released

---

[56] For example Donaldson, *Piers Plowman*, 186–7; Frank, *Piers Plowman*, 86 n. 9.
[57] ST, I.1.10 ad 3.

to man through Christ's Passion and victory. At that stage he is seen in close connection with the Apostolic power granted to the Church; there he appears as the one who consecrates the Eucharistic food. But in XVI.36-9 the dreamer is not yet in a position to come at these notions. Instead Piers makes a statement which if set against the context of Passus XIX may seem elliptical. We must not, however, confuse the two contexts or try to read the second into the first. It seems to me that XVI.36-9 gives Will a compressed figure whose implications can only be unfolded in the ensuing poetic narrative. The dreamer will only be able to reach the Piers of Passus XIX (enigmatically suggested in XVI.36-9) through following the very creation of Piers's "power". We readers must follow the dreamer in this process of understanding the allegory, and should not reduce this to an exegete's atemporal picture model.

Despite such hints towards the saving Sacramental Powers (Penance and Eucharist—XVI.36-9), there is an ominous aspect as well. Piers says, through such "power of owre pryne Iesu . . . I saue it til I se it rypen and somdel y-fruited" (XVI.37; 38). The qualifiers we must note are "somdel" and "til". What will happen after it is ripe and "somdel y-fruited", and why only "somdel"? The vision faces these questions, and they are central. When we reach that later part we must remember the threatening undertone of this earlier passage, and we must surely cast out all the exegesis of those critics who insist that Langland is portraying the *lignum vitae* of Genesis 2.9 or Apocalypse 22.2. The fruit of the *lignum vitae* is the fruit of achieved salvation. But here, besides the dark undertones already mentioned, and developed later on, the tree is attacked by the World, Flesh and Fiend (XVI.27-49). All is dramatic activity, change and mutability around the tree. The fruit grows and ripens although it is sometimes prevented from this by adversaries. There is a desperate energy needed to protect the tree, even to let the fruit "rypen" and become "somdel y-fruited". Such action is more appropriate to the terrestrial sphere of time present, with all its chances and changes, than to the Paradise where the *lignum vitae* and its fruit of achieved salvation grow. (Nor is "somdel" appropriate to the latter.) Later we will come to the lines where the fruit falls and is taken to "*lymbo inferni*" and this too refutes the exegesis that the tree is the tree of Life, but the matter is not worth raising explicitly again. Those critics who choose to transplant Langland's tree into a pleasant "Biblical milieu" and then turn it into an exegete's picturing model, simply ignore Langland's poetic domination of words and images, his own creation of nuances and discriminations in his own handling of allegorical modes.

The defence against that "wykked wynde", the World, is structured similarly to the defence against the "fel wynde" of the Flesh, already discussed. Piers tells the dreamer that against this wind he uses the first prop, "that is, *potencia-Dei-Patris*" (XVI.30). Again "that is" alerts the dreamer, and reader, to remember that he is meeting metaphor. Robertson and Huppé say that this prop, "by implication, produces the fear of the Lord".[58] They give no reasons for this inference but I believe they are justified in drawing it. This is because of the parallel structure with the use of the second prop. The metaphoric use of the first prop draws on the effects of the power created through the Incarnate acts of the *sapiencia-Dei-patris*. And the effects of the consciousness of God's power on man, tempted by the "faire siʒtes", will be to produce "the fear of the Lord". As Psalm 110.10, Proverbs 1.7, and Ecclesiasticus 1.16 make it clear, the fear of the Lord is the beginning of Wisdom and Knowledge— Proverbs 14.27 even claims "the fear of the Lord is a fountain of life, to depart from the snare of death." So the dreamer sees in Piers an agent to activate the effects of the power of God the Father, at this point. Piers is thus perceived as the active barrier between man's development and various "Temptations" which imperil it. He is the barrier in so far as he is mediator for the effects of the power and wisdom of God which are available to man.

With the use of the third prop in Langland's allegory the vexed question of the unintelligible "division of labour" arises. First it is made perfectly clear by both Anima and Piers that *Liberum Arbitrium* is inextricably associated with Piers in his role of the tree's and gar-den's farmer (XVI.16–XVII.47). There is actually *no* statement that we are to read off a rigorous "division of labour". Quite the oppo-site in fact: Piers is viewed as a superior who is essential to *Liberum Arbitrium's* farming. Secondly, the treatment of the first two props has shown us how Piers is also viewed as the necessary mediator, through whose actions the dreamer focuses the divine power opened to man. The dreamer, the reader, and *Liberum Arbitrium* are all at this stage dependent on the focal figure of Piers, the visionary mediator through whom we expect to come to Christ, "*Petrus, id est, Christus*". Bearing these facts in mind, we can approach Passus XVI.40–52.

When, with the powers Piers can mediate, the tree has been preserved to become "somdel y-fruited", the Fiend himself attacks:

> And thanne fondeth the Fende my fruit to destruye,
> With all the wyles that he can and waggeth the rote,
> And casteth vp to the croppe vnkynde neighbores,
> Bakbiteres breke-cheste brawleres and chideres,
> And leith a laddre there-to of lesynges aren the ronges,
> And feccheth away my floures sumtyme afor both myn eyhen.
>
> (XVI.40–5)

---

[58] *Piers Plowman*, 193.

Superficially a reader might assume that this is one of those literalizing picture models we found in Deguileville. In evidence he might point to the ladder whose rungs are "lesynges", and the missiles who are "vnkynde neighbores". Perhaps such assumptions lie vaguely behind D. Mills's scorn of those and similar images in this passage.[59] But we must stress "superficially", because the image is active and proves intractable to being read as a picture model. It should be noticed that the Fiend is not depicted as a wind, but as an agent in the same mode as Piers. He is shown as animate, active, choosing evil. He is the one, we will later hear, who first beguiled and perverted man's *Liberum Arbitrium* and his cultivation (XVIII.284 ff.). But, orthodoxly enough, Langland believes that man's lapsed state was chosen by his own "Free Arbitration" and his ensuing temptations are always directed towards his own "Free Arbitration".[60] So when the Fiend himself is imaged in action, "with all the wyles that he can", the dreamer will at some point see that man's own judgement is challenged to make a choice, for in this kind of attack it seems to him man's own will is fully exposed. Langland's Fiend-propelled "vnkynde neighbores" are capable of nipping off spiritual growth well before any charitable fruition (XV.45).[61] They are thus worthy of the Fiend. Piers's apparent inaction at this stage of the allegory also emphasises *Liberum Arbitrium's* own role, while Piers has to watch the Fiend and his missiles stealing off "my floures sumtyme afor bothe myn eyhen" (XVI.45). Even at his point man's free choice, although "Vnder Piers the Plowman", can and will lose touch with the Divine Vision, the mediating lens, embodied in Piers. The poetry in XVI.40–5 surely communicates a sense of the Fiend's immediacy to the process of growth, and conveys his energy in a far more impressive way than the poetry of the first two attacks even attempted. Thus he "waggeth,/and casteth vp to the croppe vnkynde neighbores", he "leith a laddre thre-to" and he "feccheth away my floures". This distinction is apt, for only through the animate Fiend and man's false choices could the World and the Flesh have become "wykked" and "fel".

Even in this attack, we should observe, *Liberum Arbitrium* acts only "by leue of my-selue", just as all along he is "Vnder Piers the Plowman". Here too *Liberum Arbitrium's* defence will be conditioned by the use of the effects of the first two props which we have just noted. Langland is also suggesting how against the active Fiend, man's "Liberum Arbitrium", in St Thomas Aquinas's words, "is cause

---

[59] In *Piers Plowman: Critical Approaches*, ed. Hussey, 202–4.
[60] See *City of God*, XIII.14–15, XIV.3,6.
[61] Compare *Inferno* 28.34–42, for the sin's gravity.

of its own movement: because through free will [liberum arbitrium] man moves himself to act".[62] This is why the dreamer is told:

> Ac *Liberum-Arbitrium* letteth hym some tyme,
> That is lieutenant to loken it wel be leue of my-selue;
>
> (XVI.46–7)

We notice the precarious quality of "some tyme". When does Liberum Arbitrium elect not to resist the Fiend? The consequences of such a choice are pointed out in XVI.45, where human development is curtailed before fruition, and so the Fiend "sumtyme" wins. Passus XVI.50–52 implies that *Liberum Arbitrium* now has access to the third prop, the effects of the grace of the Holy Spirit; therefore any failure to exploit this against the Devil may lay man open to the Latin sentences following line 47: "qui peccat in spiritum sanctum, numquam remittetur . . . qui peccat per liberum arbitrium non repugnat". The consequences are the irremissible sin again the Spirit.[63] The first part of our question, at what "tyme" does *Liberum Arbitrium* not resist, has another answer too. This we will come to when the fruit falls, but it should be pointed out now that man's free choice can obviously no longer work in the time of *death*.

Piers emphasises to the dreamer that the power of grace and the Holy Spirit are available if man chooses well (XVI.48–52). These lines too have troubled Donaldson and others, not only on account of the supposed "division of labour", but also because the critics ask why Langland should think grace is "exclusively the attribute of the Holy Ghost".[64] First we should conclude the discussion about the problems of the "division of labour" by recalling that there is no evidence for a simple "division of labour", and furthermore that throughout the passage Anima and Piers both insist that *Liberum Arbitrium* and Piers are in close association. We have seen how delicately and precisely Langland suggests this interdependence up to XVI.47, and have understood why Piers tells the dreamer that he leaves defence against the Fiend to his "lieutenant" *Liberum Arbitrium*. Passus XVI.48–52 now fuses all three aggressors into one attack of the "pouke". Piers's strategy here is to offer a recapitulation for us and the dreamer. It also helps to guard us against making an overliteralistic "division of labour". The fruit is still called Piers's fruit (XVI.49), just as it will be called "Piers's fruit" at XVIII.20. The victory of *Liberum Arbitrium*, inspired by grace, is still Piers's victory as well as *Liberum Arbitrium's* (XVI.52). This recapitulation neatly

---

[62] *ST.*, I.83.1.
[63] Robertson and Huppé, *Piers Plowman*, 194–5; see Holcot on *Sapientia*, lectio XXXIX–XLI.
[64] Donaldson, *Piers Plowman*, 187 n. 4.

fuses into one image those ideas and images which Piers has dismantled for the dreamer over the last twenty-eight lines. Again we must not read Langland's images here as picture models from which we are to glean such literalistic information as a "division of labour", or to take the World, Flesh and Devil as three literally separate and independent forces.

We can now return to the question of why only *Liberum Arbitrium* is shown using the third prop. In Passus XII.61–5 Ymagynatyf told the dreamer that grace "groweth" amongst the lowly and patient, and "thorugh the gyfte of the holygoste". It is interesting that four passus before XVI the dreamer's Imagination offered an image of grace growing in the "place" of Patience, and growing as the Holy Spirit's gift. Now (XVI) the dreamer finds the image much developed but closely related to the earlier one. He still sees grace coming from the Holy Ghost, and as a gift closely associated with Patience in man (XVI.8), and once again images of growth dominate the new context. In Passus XVII the Samaritan himself claims that the Trinity only grants forgiveness of sin and grace to men through the Holy Spirit and he talks of "the grace of the holy gooste goddes owne kynde' (XVII.221–2; 270). Later, in Passus XIX.129–30 Mercy records that the Virgin Mary "conceyued thorw speche/and grace of the holy goste". In the same passus the dreamer thinks he watches "*spiritus paraclitus*" descend on Piers and the Apostles. Conscience explains to him:

> This is Crysts messager,
> An cometh fro the grete god and Grace is his name.
> (XIX.202–3)

It is clear that the gift of grace is closely associated with the activity of the Holy Spirit after Christ's Ascension. In John 16.7–16 Jesus stated that the Comforter would come only after the Son had departed, as the Spirit who was to guide men to truth. The communication of grace to men living after the Ascension is thus particularly associated for Langland with the third Person of the Trinity, and in this he is consistent. But despite this *rationale*, the poet is not giving us a clearly labelled allegorical picture from which we are to extract literalistic dogmatic propositions. In the whole context the poet has shown us the inter-dependence of *Liberum Arbitrium* and Piers, and he is just about to stress the mysterious Triune nature of the Trinity (XVI.55–63; see also XVII.138ff.). He chooses in this final image (which I have called recapitulatory and fusing) to place the emphasis on the present efficacy of grace through the Holy Spirit and on the necessary commitment of man's own *Liberum Arbitrium*, but he is not encouraging us to break down his total complex development into a single simple scale model. To do so would be an insult to Langland's own control over his allegorical process, and would falsify his own ways of thinking about religious problems.

At this point the dreamer interrupts (XVI.53). He wishes to concentrate on the image of the three props on which spiritual fruition seems dependent. The dreamer has been impressed by the apparent unity and identity of the three props: it seemed, "on o more thei growed" (XVI.55–9). His mediator agrees and assures him that "the grounde ther it groweth Goodnesse it hiʒte", and that the tree "the Trinite in meneth" (XVI.60–3). This brief section (XVI.55–63) also appears to have been maltreated by critics. Donaldson and others have maintained that these lines support a reading of the whole allegory as one concerning the pre-Christian era, because the image of the three props and their unity is "derived from the legend concerning the pre-history of the cross". I have already pointed out the weakness of any efforts to pretend that Langland writes a single "pre-Christian allegory", but it is worth examining whatever encouragement the Legends of the Cross may have given to those scholars who wish to impose the Legends' time-scheme onto Langland's.[65] In the "Story of the Holy Rood" Seth takes three kernels from the tree of the Fall. He is instructed to plant these in Adam's mouth when he dies. The three trees that grow from the kernels (cedar, cypress and pine) "bitaken the trenite". When many years later Moses and his followers come to the Vale of Ebron, Moses finds the three "wandes" and sees that they are significant:

> [they] mene
> þe trinite þam thre bitwene,
> . . .
> For in þe rote all war þai mett.

Doublesss Langland's five words, "on o more thei growed", may remind some scholars of the Legends' words, "in the rote all war þai mett'. But when this association makes them claim that Langland's images are "derived from" the Legends, we should be suspicious, for the evidence here for direct connection is inadequate. Furthermore Langland's props *seem* of one root: "to my mynde, as me thinketh . . . semen". Nor do Langland's props have any contextual parallels to the Legends' images (e.g., the Fall, the visit of Seth, the three kernels, Adam's mouth, the oil of mercy) and they are not literalized in the way the Legends' are. When such disparity is evident, any claim that Langland's images are "derived from" the Legends un-

---

[65] Donaldson, *Piers Plowman*, 186; *Legends of the Holy Rood*, EETS, 46 (1871), 62–86: following quotations from "The Story of the Holy Rood", 11. 413–14, 416 in this collection.

deniably invites arbitrary connections which lead to misinterpretation. To follow this questionable procedure by forcing Langland's time-schemes to fit the Legend of which the scholars have been reminded is an example of perverse critical irrelevance. However, if the critics only mean (by "derived from") that Langland's passage reminds them of one or two other passages in medieval poetry, then we can believe this record of their mental associations and knowledge without being obliged to make Langland's writing fit the contexts of which they are reminded.[66] Langland's images, however, cannot be put into substantial and significant correlation with the Legends'; the latter, it follows, must not be used as a gloss on Langland. Besides this, there is the question of poetic modes. We have followed the compressed, complexly evocative movement of Langland's imagery so far in this passage, and found that we cannot reduce his writing here to the unanimity of exegetical picturing models. But this is exactly what such critics do: they destroy Langland's carefully developed context, diminish his images to the "ping-pong" of the homilists and for good measure they impose the Legends' own simple time-scheme. So although Piers says, "the Trinite it meneth", and a Legend says that the wands "mene/the trinite", there remains a crucial modal and conceptual differentiation between the two contexts. It is significant that Langland follows Piers's "it meneth" with these words:

> And egrelich he loked on me and ther-fore I spared
> To asken hym any more there-of
>
> (XVI.64–5)

There is no attempt to pin down the insight any further, at this point. Now the model must be left and the dreamer, for once, accepts the position. Perhaps Piers's looking "egrelich" suggests the hope that a disclosure around the images of the Trinity will have occurred, enlightening the dreamer. Piers hopes, as Ramsey would say, that "the penny will drop, the ice break, the light dawn". But the disclosure has not yet occurred for the dreamer.[67] All this should clarify how we must continually be aware of Langland's concern with his own allegorical context. If he too was reminded of the Legends of the Cross, he chose not to use their contexts, not to imitate their mode, and not to use their time-scheme. Once again, the critic must stay

---

[66] On these methodological issues see two articles by Q. Skinner: "The Limits of Historical Explanation", *Philosophy*, 41 (1966), 199–215, and "Meaning and Understanding in the History of Ideas", *History and Theory*, 8 (1969), 3–53.

[67] Ramsey, *Religious Language* (London, 1957), 51; compare XVI.64–5 and the Samaritan's attempt to use a series of models to convey orthodox notions about the Trinity (XVIII.131 ff.).

alert to the *process* of Langland's figurative modes, and responsive to the particular religious intelligence they manifest.

The dreamer, we recall, had asked in Passus XV.145, "What is Charite?" and in XVI.4, "What charite is to mene". So far the fruit of the tree's growth has been regarded as imaging the product of spiritual development in which the dreamer is concerned. Therefore we are not surprised when the dreamer doggedly return to the fruit:

> and badde hym ful fayre
> To discreue the fruit that so faire hangeth.
> (XVI.65–6)

Piers attempts to convey a distinction about degrees of Charity in living, using the image of the fruit on the tree and the parallel degrees of chastity.[68] The dreamer, still intent on discovering Charity, asks Piers:

> to pulle adown an apple and he wolde,
> And suffre me to assaye what sauoure it hadde.
> (XVI.73–4)

Here it is probably necessary to comment on an interpretation already mentioned: that the allegory at this stage is one of the Fall.[69] This does not prove a relevant reading, I think, because it is another instance of arbitrary connections which are then offered as strict explanations of the text in question. Here Langland is not attempting to communicate the nature and effects of the time when "Adam and Eue eten apples vnrosted" (V.612), when Adam was "put fram blisse" (XI.409), and

> Coueytise to kunne and to know science
> Putte oute of paradys Adam and Eue
> (XV.61–2)

A time when Adam:

> Frette of that fruit and forsoke, as it were,
> The loue of owre lorde and his lore bothe,
> And folwed that the fende tauȝte and his felawes wille,

---

[68] XVI.3, 9, 29, 39, 40, 49: Smith outlines the commonplace association of charity and chastity in *Traditional Imagery of Charity in Piers Plowman*, 38–40, 67–9.

[69] Already mentioned in note 40 to this chapter, see references there, adding Bloomfield, review in *Spec*, 37 (1962), 121, 123

A3eines resoun . . .

(XVIII.194–6)

So he brought, "a sikenesse to vs alle" (V.490). The main reason for
denying that Langland was trying to embody such comments in
Passus XVI is that there is no contextual attempt to suggest that
the tree here is to be thought of as that forbidden tree. My analysis
should have established this by now. There is also the further
objection that there could be no suggestion that the three states of
"Wydwehode", "Matrimognie" and "Maydenhode" (XVI.68–77),
with their varying degrees of charity, might exist before the Fall.
Besides this, there is no "Wydwehode" without Death, and there
was, in Christian belief, no Death without the Fall and sin (Romans
5.12). Nor do the proponents of the Fall reading state in what way
the dreamer's intense search for the meaning of Charity is at this stage
so reminiscent of Adam's sin. Even the passing references to the
Fall which have just been quoted from *Piers Plowman* itself, show
that the poet was well aware of its momentous nature; it is most
improbable that he would ignore the ramifications and particular
nuances of the acts of Adam and Eve were he trying to concentrate
our attention on that Fall, having shown his concern for them in
passing. Nor does the passage in Passus XVI seem to suggest Genesis
3.6–9 in any way. It is strange that Fowler and his supporters should
see Piers and the dreamer acting the parts of "mulier" and her
beguiled man. But perhaps the most damaging aspect of their reading
is the general one: that it simply destroys the poet's total context with
its own peculiar discriminations and images, a totality we have been
studying in detail.

When the dreamer asks his mediator to "pulle adown an apple",
the motivation in the poet's context is the question, "What is
Charite?", and "What charite is to mene" (XV.145; XVI.3). But
by this stage the poet has created so rich an imagistic context that the
question can instigate a disclosure which has to embrace time past as
well as time present. Critics have of course commented on how
Piers "shaking the tree sends us straight into the 'historical past' of
the Biblical narrative". But even where they accept its coherence
they have chosen not to attempt a discussion of the details of poetic-
logic in this "multiple-time allegory"—doubtless because the transi-
tion seems in itself so imaginatively powerful and satisfactory.[70] But
it is this I shall now examine, studying how the poet's modes can
handle the temporal dimension so crucial to the theology of Christian
allegory. For contrast, we should remember Deguileville's attempts
(considered in chapter three) to handle salvation history in his own

---

[70] See especially Elizabeth Salter, *Piers Plowman*, 76

allegory centred on tree images. We can also bear in mind Frank's and Donaldson's conviction that Langland is in dire "confusion".

The "shewynge" (XVI.1; 21) with which the dreamer has been privileged has gradually moved from Piers's vivid description, report and instruction (XVI.25–52; 60–63) to what seems to the dreamer a more immediate representation of the images (XVI.57–9; 67–72). This movement culminates in the allegorical images becoming involved in space and time. We see Piers respond to the dreamer's desire, now in action: "And Pieres caste to the croppe" (XVI.75). But the context created by the poet no longer allows Charity to exist as an abstraction to be taken from Anima's picture model. When the mediator would bring the fruit of Charity to the visionary Will, the fruit has already been viewed from the perspective of time present— differentiated and involved in human states of living (post-lapsarian ones too, we noted). So when the mediator tries to fulfil the dreamer's will, the dreamer is not allowed a simple answer or a simple set of propositions about Charity. The attempt to examine the fruit, to bring them to the dreamer's "sauoure", involves *action* and reveals to Will something about the existence of post-lapsarian Charity. Intimate knowledge of the fruit is only possible if they are pulled down and brought to Will. The attempt to do this causes three kinds of complaint from the three states of fruit, obliquely reflecting a traditional Christian argument that the greater the charity in a man, the less his temporal attachment.[71] Matrimony "made a foule noyse" and "gradde so reufulliche" because it partakes most fully of the temporal, and separation from its temporal commitments and place of development is the most painful (XVI.75–8). The dreamer can thus see that charity is time-strained and has no cloistered existence.

It still remains to be seen how the actions of Piers cohere to this context and how he focuses the dreamer's vision. Piers had said that the Fiend, "casteth vp to the croppe vnkynde neighbores" and so perverts natural development although "some tyme" *Liberum Arbitrium* prevents him (XVI.42–7). But now the dreamer sees "Piers caste to the croppe" (XVI.75). The echo need not lead to any impetuous equations since Piers shakes the ripe tree (which he has helped to nurture) whereas the Fiend prevented ripeness. When the Fiend and his instruments actually attack the fruit:

> Thanne *Liberum-Arbitrium* laccheth the thridde plante,
> And palleth adown the pouke purelich thorw grace
> And helpe of the holy goste and thus haue I the maystrie.
>
> (XVI.50–2)

---

[71] For example, Augustine, *On Christian* Doctrine I.3 ff.; Holcot on *Sapientia*, XXXIX, XL; Robertson, "The Doctrine of Charity . . .", *Spec*, 26 (1951). 24–49.

The earlier development showed that Piers and his "lieutenant" have the power to protect the plant from attacks, "til", says Piers, "I see it rypen and somdel y-fruited." In a post-lapsarian world this "til" is suggestive. For things that ripen, as Spenser says, "Short Time shall soon cut down with his consuming sickle" (FQ.VII.8.1). Piers has no sickle, but we have now come to the fulfilment of the dark reservations in "till" and "somdel", which I noticed earlier (XVI.39).[72] At this point the Fiend does not touch the tree of symbolic growth, but Piers's own actions and their effects unfold the qualities that have unhappily and inescapably become merged with all development. Another hint noticed earlier is also relevant. Piers quoted Ps. 36.24, "Cum ceciderit iustus, non collidetur; quia Dominus supponit manum suam" (XVI.25). Now we actually *see* that the charitable just man must indeed fall, in a post-lapsarian world. It is significant that in this falling not only does the Fiend not touch the ripe fruit, but *Liberum Arbitrium* is not there to hinder its falling, and Piers does not attempt to preserve the ripened fruit on the tree of growth; quite the contrary. In *Paradise Lost* Michael tells Adam that in his own post-lapsarian life, "So maist thou live, till like ripe fruit thou drop" (PL.XI.535), and it seems clear that Piers is forcefully focusing our vision on this naked fact, necessarily accompanying even the growth of justice and charity. Because in orthodox Christian doctrine we are fallen, Langland implies that even the just man is deformed with original sin.[73] Thus:

> For euere as thei dropped adown the deuel
> was redy,
> And gadred hem alle togideres
> . . .
> Bar hem forth boldely no body hym letted,
> (XVI.79–80; 83)

The Devil takes them into "*lymbo inferni*" (XVI.84). The poet's emphasis, that "no body hym letted" may confirm my commentary on the significance of *Liberum Arbitrium's* absence at this stage and on the way Piers makes no effort to keep the fruit on the tree. As the Psalm Piers himself quoted maintains, the just shall fall.

The verse Piers quoted does also contain a promise for the just: "non collidetur; quia Dominus supponit manum suam". And yet at this point the dreamer's vision shows the charitable and just fruit irrevocably taken into the Devil's power: "There is darkenesse and drede and the deuel maister" (XVI.85). A great contrast indeed to the

---

[72] Langland develops this aspect in the C-text figure of Elde.
[73] N. P. Williams, *The Ideas of the Fall and of Original Sin* (London, 1927), chapters I–VI.

position where the tree's growth and fruition allows Piers to say, "thus haue I the maystrie" (XVI.52). How then is the promise of the Psalm justified?

This is where the poet must disclose the theological basis of his religious vocabulary. To do this he bursts out of the time present of the fourteenth-century visionary.[74] For the poet this involves continuing the development of the fruit image already noted; in two lines omitted just above, the fruit is seen as:

> Adam and Abraham and Ysay the prophete,
> Samson and Samuel and seynt Iohan the baptiste.
>
> (XVI.81–2)

If the dreamer and readers are to see how although the fruit falls God will not let it be utterly cast down (XVI.25), they must be shown the *process* by which the powers of the props become available to Piers and *Liberum Arbitrium*, and especially how they may be effective in fulfilling the promise of Psalm 36.24, even after the fruit ripens and falls. The very grounds for the means of grace and the poet's hope of salvation must be disclosed, and this without ignoring death and evil. So to understand the present possibilities for the present, the poet must shatter the time-bonds that constrict the imagination. And this is the point where the falling fruit of time present, ripe in charity, suddenly give place to those just men from Adam to John, the prophet who prepared the way of Christ, and then baptised him. For the hope of deliverance in time present is only viable if man can credit that the hope rests on a deliverance effected within human history—and in such a way that the effects of that past deliverance may still be present.

The action which is to disclose the poet's grounds of faith is instigated by the focusing figure, the mediating symbol of the present vision—Piers:

> And Pieres for pure tene that o pile he lauȝte,
> And hitte after hym happe how it myȝte,
> *Filius*, bi the Fader wille and frenesse of
> *Spiritus Sancti*,
> To go robbe that raggeman and reue the fruit
> fro hyme.
>
> (XVI.86–9)

Earlier in Passus XVI when Piers had been describing the powers available to present men, he had related the use of the second prop,

---

[74] Elizabeth Salter, *Piers Plowman*, 76.

"the passioun and the power of owre prynce Iesu", and we mentioned his function in the poet's dramatic present in bringing "goddes passioun in mynde" (XVI.37; 38). Now Piers instigates a re-enactment of the *way* in which the second prop came to men's desperate need, and the way he can, and does, bring this into men's minds. So Piers the mediating symbol is also re-constructing the generation of his own present power and role. This is one of the occasions when we must be especially careful to avoid slipping into the exegetes' habit of assuming that allegory is necessarily a picturing model. If we do slip, then we will be led to make statements such as the following: "Piers stands for God the Father."[75] We are not to materialize, freeze and literalize the figure of Piers into a picture model from which we read off such statements. I cannot find that Langland's writing here gives any encouragement to such assumptions and readings. Through the vision's mediator we focus on the "moment" when the Trinity (XVI.88) determines that the second Person is "to go robbe that raggeman and reue the fruit fro hym" (XVI.89). This focus immediately brings us to those saving events in time past, launched by the Annunciation and Incarnation:

> And thanne spakke *Spiritus Sanctus* in Gabrieles mouthe
> To a mayde that hiʒte Marye a meke thing with-alle,
> That one Iesus, a Iustice sone moste Iouke in her chambre,
> Tyl *plenitudo temporis* . . .
>
> (XVI.90–3)

Time past comes directly to our present vision, and Langland creates what Milton suggested (and achieved) in his own poem "On the Morning of Christ's Nativity":

> For if such holy Song
> Enwrap our fancy long,
> Time will run back, and fetch the age of gold
> (ll.132–5)

The age of gold is the Messianic time and during Passus XVI–XIX its effects and nature will be explored and re-discovered.[76] It is here that we will see how the "fruit" is recovered, and how, in some earlier words of the poet, Christ "blewe all thi blissed in-to the blisse of paradise" (V.503). That will not be part of the vision until the

---

[75] Donaldson, *Piers Plowman*, 184.
[76] See Rosemond Tuve, *Images and Themes in Five Poems by Milton* (Cambridge, Mass., 1957), 60.

dreamer/poet sees Christ himself become the "first fruits of them that sleep", and all mankind brought to life (1 Corinthians 15.20–3; see Passus XVIII–XIX). This "shewynge" moves from allegorical imagery into direct vision accommodated to the mental and imaginative capacities of the dreamer, and it is the figure Piers who has put Will on this way, a way apprehended through the concentration and control of the poet's own allegorical medium.

This concludes the study of the tree of Charity, and of its critics, but it is worth extending the reading by eleven lines. Here the poet, or dreamer senses that when Jesus could have challenged the Fiend as an infant:

> Pieres the Plowman parceyued plenere tyme,
> And lered hym lechecrafte his lyf for to saue
> That though he were wounded with his enemye to
> warisshe hym-self;
>
> (XVI.103–5)

This passage has caused much difficulty.[77] R. E. Kaske tried to resolve the difficulties by using Luke 2.40ff. and medieval exegetes (those solve-alls) on Luke 4. Here the exegetes see Christ the physician being taught by the Holy Ghost, in so far as Christ is man. Then Kaske adds that John the Baptist baptising Christ is equal to John "teaching Christ" (why?) and sees, "John as God's grace, here obviously suggesting the grace of the Holy Ghost by which Christ is taught after His baptism". He then uses Hugh of St Cher on Luke 7.19–22, where the thirteenth-century exegete comments that "mystically, John the Baptist is baptismal grace." Kaske relates all this exegesis on St Luke's words to *Piers Plowman* by supposing "a complex relationship between Piers and John the Baptist". But unfortunately this is also a relationship too tenuous, arbitrary, and extra-literary to carry weight. It is typical of modern efforts to imitate medieval exegesis and it is inappropriate because there is no certainty that Langland is at this point writing the kind of images and models which should be treated in the exegetes' way.[78] Nor is Piers the kind of figure from whom we can read off information or propositions like, Piers "is baptismal grace"—even if we qualify it with *mystice*. Instead of hurrying to our concordances and dictionaries of exegetical allegories, we should ask whether the poet has written anything relevant to this passage anywhere else in the same verbal structure. I believe he has. In Passus XVIII Peace explains to the other Daughters of God that God set Adam "in solace and in souereigne

---

[77] For example, Donaldson, *Piers Plowman*, 186
[78] Kaske, in *Critical Approaches*, ed. Bethurum, 42–8.

myrthe", although he allowed him to know sin and sorrow. But afterwards:

> god auntred hym-self and toke Adames kynde,
> To wyte what he hath suffred in thre sondri places,
> Both in heuene and in erthe and now til helle he
> thynketh,
> To wite what al wo is . . .
>
> (XVIII.220–3)

God became man to learn and experience. This striking notion seems to bear on the difficult passage in Passus XVI, but before analysing the relationship, the relevance of some other passages should be noticed.[79] In Passus XVI itself the Samaritan tells the dreamer that the Son acts as "a mene" to the father by which God can "knowe his owne myȝte", and also know the suffering "of hym and of his seruant and what thei suffre bothe" (XVI.192–3). He also says that the Son became a creature to *learn* what it is to be a creature. He drives home this paradox powerfully, using Christ's own words from the Cross:

> *Deus meus, deus meus, ut quid dereliquisti me?*
> That is, creatour wex creature to knowe what was bothe;
>
> (XVI.214–5)

Thus Christ the Creator in his manhood *learns* the desolation of the believing creature who finds himself cut off from his Creator. And in Passus XIX Conscience explains that "owre lord prynce Iesus" only took on a conqueror's role when "he gan to wexe / In the manere of a man", learning like a conqueror, "to knowe many sleightes" (XIX.92–7). It is clear that this notion of the Creator become creature to learn the existential situation of his creatures, is one which fascinated the poet.[80]

Turning back to Passus XVI we recall that Piers "parceyued plenere tyme, / And lered hym lechecrafte . . .". Kaske is right to observe that the passage concerns Christ in his Manhood—the passage makes that obvious enough. But the *Deus-homo* is guided from fighting the devil prematurely (from a premature exertion of his full Godhead), and he is also guided in the "lechecrafte" that will enable him "his lyf for to saue" (however gravely wounded),

---

[79] In this way I hope to avoid a charge I have made against other critics—of putting forward arbitrary associations as relevant elucidation of various passages.

[80] Behind Langland's development of "creatour wexe creature", there surely lies the idea of *kenosis* in Philippians 2.7. Perhaps Langland's thinking here could be fruitfully connected with Pascal's *Mystery of Jesus* as read by L. Goldmann, *The Hidden God* (London, 1964), 78–80.

leading to his acclaim as "leche of lyf" (XVIII.118). And he is guided by Piers. The guidance Jesus receives harmonizes with the poet's emphasis (in the other passages just quoted) that the Creator in his Incarnation is obliged to learn creaturely limitation, and to learn from a creaturely perspective. Although it is certainly an elliptical figure we must, as usual, avoid literalizing Piers into a fixed counter. So far we have found that Piers acts as the saving and teaching agent appropriate to men's perception and vision at particular stages. But Jesus's perception must be oriented towards discerning his role as *Christus Medicus*, Suffering Servant (XVI.192–3) and *Christus Victor* (XVIII). If Jesus is to fulfil his mission and save "his lyf", then his vision will need to focus on the right way and timing. It is as this focusing lens that Piers (who "parceyued plenere tyme") functions in Jesus's own spiritual development.[81] Very characteristically Langland lets the dreamer perceive figuratively in this inner vision a notion which he will come to again and again as he discloses aspects of the Christian paradox that the "creatour wex creature". Certainly we should not confuse Langland's figures here with the very different modes of expression found in exegesis and homiletics, and I hope my analysis of the tree of Charity has demonstrated that Langland's modes, at this point, give a critic no cause for such confusions.

III

In the episode we have just studied Langland's presentation of the Incarnation turned on the careful introduction of temporal dimensions into his allegory. The passage superseded the figurative mode which depends mainly on picturing models and we saw how his allegory must be understood in terms of process. I shall now extend the discussion to describe the way Langland articulates another area of agricultural imagery. Although such imagery is recurrent, it is concentrated in Passus V–VII and XIX as well as in the one we have just examined. Scholars have offered much advice about reading Langland's ploughing imagery, and Robertson and Huppé apply their habitual method. As soon as they meet the word "plow" (Prologue, 20) they flee from Langland to allegorical-exegetical dictionaries, asserting that "conventional Scriptural exposition gives the

---

[81] Milton's *Paradise Regained* shows Jesus only gradually becoming aware of the precise nature of his vocation; his uncertainty is a necessary part of his temptations and his development. This process seems relevant to Langland's approach in the passage under discussion. On the relevant theological basis, see T. F. Torrance, "The Place of Christology in Biblical and Dogmatic Theology", in *Essays in Christology for Karl Barth*, ed. T. H. L. Parker (London, 1956), 18. On Milton's treatment of the problem, Barbara K. Lewalski, *Milton's Brief Epic* (London, 1966), especially part two.

plowman a unique symbolic significance". They look up what exegetes have to say about Luke 9.62, Luke 17.7, Ecclesiasticus 38.26, 1 Corinthians 9.10, and, inevitably, they turn to Raban Maur's dictionary of symbols. After this exercise they conclude that "plowing" is always a symbol "for the exercise of the prelatical life".[82] So when they reach the agricultural Passus (V–VII) we know what to expect. At his first entrance Piers is definitely "the true pastor" who "represents the tradition of the ideal of the good plowmen, the producers of spiritual food: the patriarchs, the prophets, Christ, St Peter, the apostles, the disciples and those of their followers who actually fulfil the ideal of the prelatical life."[83] Having extracted "producers of spiritual food" from the dictionary's "plowmen" and applied the abstraction to Langland's working ploughman, it follows automatically that when Piers organizes the work on the half acre the critics employ familiar exegetical procedures to read VI.20–2 as a figurative statement that Langland's ploughmen are all "planting virtues among the folk". The actions of Piers himself, they decide, "will supply spiritual food" to all the workers (see XVI, 17–21), and when Piers makes a conventional will before his planned pilgrimage (VI.85–104) the critics make such readings as the following: the "tythe" of Piers's "corne and catel", which he has actually given to the Church, "represents the fruit of Piers's pastoral labour".[84] In elucidating Piers's actions the scholars find two passages especially relevant, one from Gregory's *Moralia*, where the "Agricolae" are interpreted as preachers of the Church, and one from Bede where sowing in a field is read as sowing "in his heart"; for, according to Robertson and Huppé "Piers plants the virtues in the hearts of the folk while they are at work preparing themselves."[85] Indeed, most of Langland's imagery is apparently written in such picture models. For instance, exegizing VI.135–40, the critics comment:

the water, the opposite of the honey of sapientia, is "dulcedo hujus vitae". [*cf.* "Peter Lombard on Ps. 80.15 . . . and on Ps.123.2 . . ."]. The blind the lame and the imprisoned are those who are caught in the world but who desire spiritual food. ["On the blind see Luke 18.35ff. and Bede, *PL*.92.558. . . . For the chained

---

[82] *Piers Plowman*, 17–19: for a trenchant criticism of these scholars' treatment of the Prologue see Donaldson, in *Critical Approaches*, ed. D. Bethurum, 8–11. Robertson and Huppé give no reason for their extremely narrow selection of materials in interpreting the whole poem: it never occurs to them that social history must be relevant to an attempt at overall interpretation of the poem. This failure is of course characteristic of most criticism but it needs remedy.

[83] *Piers Plowman*, 75, see to 77.

[84] ibid., 79, 80, 82.

[85] ibid., 83.

see Ps. 68.33 and *Glossa Ordinaria PL.*113 950 . . ."]. . . . Their wheaten bread is the body of Christ, and their drink is the wine of the sacrament; in other words they receive the spiritual food of the word of God.[86]

Robertson and Huppé can therefore find absolutely no development in the agricultural imagery of *Piers Plowman* from the Prologue to Passus XX.[87] I have reported their interpretation rather fully because they represent, as I have said before, one of the two poles between which medieval criticism of figurative writing flows, and because of their real affinity with the practice of medieval exegetes, preachers and some poets previously discussed.

At the other "pole", Frank has also considered Passus V–VII. He insists that "the scene is to be read literally" and refers to Robertson and Huppé's interpretation: "I cannot accept this or their other 'allegorical' readings of the poem."[88] Unfortunately Frank is not interested enough in figurative modes to explain precisely why Robertson and Huppé's readings are so unacceptable. It is certainly curious that however "literally" he claims to read the poem, at Piers's first entry he writes, "Piers the Plowman, the symbol of man's semidivine nature". If the central figure of the scene is so obviously a "symbol", then one wonders why Frank is quite *so* dismissive of Robertson and Huppé's "symbolical interpretation".[89] When Frank comes to Passus XIX he admits that we have "an extended metaphor of plowing, sowing, and harvesting", but he is not concerned enough about allegory or "extended metaphor" to develop any close analysis of the figurative modes employed or to consider the relations between Passus XIX and V–VII.[90] We need not pursue scholarly interpretations of this area any further for the moment, since the same kinds of disagreement and confusions preside here as over the wider area of medieval figurative writing which we have been studying.[91] I have argued that any reading of figurative poetry must remain especially alert to the modes with which the poet guides the reader's approaches. We shall now see whether awareness of this fundamental demand can help us come to terms with the poetry in this agricultural area of *Piers Plowman*, and with its modern exegetes.

---

[86] *ibid.*, 83–4.

[87] *ibid.*, 222, see 221 ff.

[88] Frank, *Piers Plowman*, 23 n. 7; a more sensitive development of this line in Elizabeth Kirk, *The Dream Thought of Piers Plowman*, 72–5.

[89] Frank, *Piers Plowman*, 23 n. 7.

[90] *ibid.*, 103.

[91] Some more examples of confusion over the agricultural imagery in V–VII, XIX are found in Barbara Raw, "Piers and the Image of God in Man", in *Piers Plowman: Critical Approaches*, ed. Hussey, 145, 149, 178, where it seems that the images of Passus VI are "to be understood literally", and yet are "metaphor" of the same kind as those of XIX with "an allegorical meaning".

As a brief preliminary I shall present a few examples of standard figurative uses of argicultural imagery. Such a preface should help to make plain the peculiarity of the literary modes I attribute to Langland—peculiar, that is, when seen alongside dominant medieval figurative practice—and it can be very brief because Robertson and Huppé's summary of normal medieval procedure here (quoted above) is accurate. In a commentary on the Book of Ruth, chapter two, Stephen Langton discusses the reaping in the fields of Booz: he reads Booz as Christ, Ruth as the pure and simple student disciple. The mode can be illustrated from the exegete's comment on verse five where Booz asks, "Whose maid is this?":

Whose maid is this? Whenever anyone carefully collects the ears of corn, that is the meaning [sententias] of the Sacred Page, the Lord [Dominus] inquires after the standing of that person from the reapers, that is, from the doctors [of theology]; . . . *And Booz said*, Christ [*Et ait Boaz, Christus*] . . .[92]

Like Robertson and Huppé the medieval exegete treats the agricultural imagery and the actors as a series of figurative picture models. Such proceedings were so normal that when Jacques de Vitry delivered a sermon "to husbandmen, vinedressers and other workers", in which he exhorts his literal audience as literal *agricolae* and *operarii* to work materially, to pay tithes and to keep the Sabbath, he begins by speaking of the duty to sow "spiritual seed in the hearts of the audience" and to cultivate "the land of the church": from the field, of man's heart, is expected the fruit, that is, the word of God.[93]

The mode and the specific readings are so common that we can pass on to one of those allegorical dictionaries, so popular in the later Middle Ages and so favoured by some modern exegetes of medieval literature. The dictionary referred to here is a thirteenth-century one compiled in England. Since we are concerned with a "felde ful of folke" as the basis of the agricultural activity in *Piers Plowman* we may look under the heading, "Concerning the material field and the spiritual field". The various material fields turn out to be "spiritually" significant in many ways, and here are examples of the symbolizing mode followed:

---

[92] My translation from Beryl Smalley's edition in "Studies on the Commentaries of Cardinal Stephen Langton", G. Lacombe and B. Smalley, *AHDLMA*, 5 (1931), 1–220, see 100–1

[93] Sermon 50, ed J.-T. Welter, *L'Exemplum dans la Littérature Religieuse et Didactique au Moyen Age* (Paris, 1927), Appendix I, 457–8. See examples in *The Book of Vices and Virtues*, EETS, 217 (1942), 93–7; the Prior of Norwich's letter in W. A. Pantin, *The English Church in the Fourteenth Century* (Cambridge, 1955), 176; *The South English Legendary*, EETS, 235 (1951), 1–2.

The field is the universal church
The field is the human body
The field is the world
The field is the wild [inculta] heathen
The field is the office of preachers or preaching itself. . . .
The field of a lazy man is a people placed under a negligent prelate . . .
Morally the field of a lazy man is the vice of sloth.[94]

The images are taken as picturing models, and the dictionary form is very suitable. It highlights the irrelevance, in this figurative aesthetic, of any notions of generative process or contextual control of symbols. While examining Langland's modes in Passus V–VII and XIX we should not forget the kind of writing that dominated medieval allegory.

The subject has become confused enough to demand that we once again proceed in detail and at a slow pace. Because of this it seems sensible to head the analysis with a sketch of the general conclusions reached. In Passus V–VII the poet has created a context for imagery which was customarily read allegorically, in anything remotely resembling a religious work, and was usually part of doctrinal and ethical picture models. But in his own process he chooses to show the imagery surprisingly deprived of its habitual implications, and I shall discuss how and why Langland did this. After Passus VI he uses the figurative potential of the images slightly although he also continues to subdue it. The break-through, as it were, results from the actions and the stage instigated in Passus XVI, which I have already considered. The Incarnation, life of Jesus, Passion, Resurrection, *Harrowing* of Hell and Ascension, followed by the Pentecostal gifts, release the allegorical potential of the agricultural images. The acts of Christ in time and society articulate the imagery and make men see in a new way: the dreamer's perception, and Langland may have hoped the reader's too, is transformed. Once more I will pay particular attention to contexts and the modes being employed. As for Piers, I see no reason, so far at least, for discarding the working hypothesis outlined above and used in the preceding analysis of Passus XVI.

When Piers is first seen it is by pilgrims who "blustreden forth as bestes", searching for "a corseint that men calle Treuthe" (V.521; 539). Their perception at this point is blurred, and their religion is externalized and mechanistic (V.517–43). It is important to remember this as we examine the controversial half acre scene and the actions of Piers "and his pilgrymes" (VI.107). In his first speech Piers describes his occupation in images taken from agricultural activity—

---

[94] My translation from the edition by A. Wilmart, "Un Répertoire d'Exégèse . . . du XIII°s", in *Memorial Language* (Paris, 1940), 307–46, here 313–14.

"sowe and to sette ... sede ... thresche". Dunning correctly noted that these images are given the same material status evident in the statement that Piers also served "in tailoures crafte and tynkares crafte".[95] The poet's description of the pilgrims certainly did not make us expect them to be seeing symbolic visions, and the fact that Piers places the agricultural imagery explicitly into the same mode as images of tinkers and tailors implies that the pilgrims' "gyde" (V.1) reflects their state. He does not consider or articulate the figurative potential of his images. We have seen how habitual it had become, in pious works, to read off assorted ecclesiastical and moralistic propositions from such imagery. But here the visionary poet concentrates attention on the material basis of society, and through careful control of his context reduces the images to the literal status of tinkers and tailors, refusing to fulfil any stereotyped and stock expectations. This rejection of standard allegorical methods provides something of a shock. If we follow Frank and other committedly literalistic readers we will obviously not be shockable, whereas if we imitate Robertsonians and medieval exegetes our stock expectations are so fixed that we will grind the poet's words to fit these stock responses. Neither approach is justified, and further analysis should reinforce this contention.

Piers is to be the "gyde" and he promises the pilgrims, who "blustreden forth as bestes" (V.521), "I shal wisse ȝow witterly the weye" (V.562). He first gives them a picturing model of the way to Truth and it is one worthy of any preacher, showing that familiar blend of allegory and ultra-literalism (V.568–613). He says, "this is the weye", and describes it in such figures as the following:

> Thanne shaltow come by a crofte but come thow nouȝte there-inne;
> That crofte hat Coueyte-nouȝte-mennes-catel-ne-her wyues-
> Ne none-of-her seruantes-that-noyen-hem-myȝte;
>
> (V.581–3)

The naive picture model is probably the only sort the participants can imagine or deal with at the moment.[96] It is characteristic of Langland's use of this particular mode that it is integrated into a context which gives it some kind of spiritual and dramatic significance. The mode, for Langland, is only one of many possibilities, and it belongs to particular phases.

---

[95] See V.548–56 and Dunning's shrewd review in M Aev, 24 (1955), 26.

[96] V.614–17 was discussed at the close of chapter four and these lines do suddenly break into a new mode, anticipating later developments in the poem; see Elizabeth Zeeman (Salter), ES, 11 (1950), 1–16.

Seven times in one hundred and thirty-three lines the word "way" re-echoes.[97] Later in the poem the dreamer implies that Moses searching for Christ is going "the riȝte way" (XVI.273; XVII.5–13). The reader will have heard that Jesus said, "I am the way, and the truth, and the life. No man cometh to the Father, but by me" (John 14.6), but when the pilgrims stumble across Piers, "there was wyȝte non so wys the *wey* thider couthe" (V.520, my italics). From a Christian standpoint their position is thus desperate. Besides this and the limitations of Piers's model we also notice that the half acre scene does not seem to be the "way", to pilgrims, Piers or, finally, the poet:

> I have an half-acre to erye bi the heighe way;
> Hadde I eried this half-acre and sowen it after,
> I wolde wende with ȝow and the way teche.
>
> (VI.4–6)

The poet is not simply making a "polemical point" against pilgrimages, nor is it true that in the half acre scene he merely "substitutes an allegorical pilgrimage for a real one".[98] It seems to me that the half acre scene is neither "the way" nor an "allegorical substitute"; while it certainly comes to be regarded as a "substitute", it is generated in accordance with the capacities of the pilgrims and the poet's version of the material roots and tensions of his society. We find the same startling suppression of figurative potential already noted in Piers's first speech. Christ is not yet seen as "the way", the figure who later harrows hell is not yet directly met.[99] Piers and the pilgrims do not even undertake the "way" he himself pictured in Passus V. Instead they all focus their vision on "lyflode", "clothes", "flesche and bred", and Piers gives his assent (VI.10–21).[100]

In VI.23 there may be a pun on "teme" (theme, lesson, and also team of oxen). The knight offers Piers, the ploughman, physical help

---

[97] V.520, 540, 562, 568; VI.1, 4, 6.

[98] See J. Burrow, "The Action of Langland's Second Vision", *EC*, 15 (1965), 247–56; but Dunning's view also seems not quite accurate when he says the half acre "must be ploughed before the pilgrimage begins", *Piers Plowman* (London, 1937), 127.

[99] Barbara Raw comes near to developing this argument in her study of "Piers and the Image of God in Man", in *Piers Plowman: Critical Approaches*, ed. Hussey, 143–79; unfortunately she imposes a rather rigid OT–NT time-scheme onto the poem, necessitating some awkward explaining away: see 163–4, for example, which squares oddly with Passus V.597, 602, 604, 612, 614, 644–7, let alone 614–17. She is certainly aware of these self-made difficulties (164) but they remain (see 143–7, 149–50, 154–5, 161).

[100] "Flesshe and bred" would be pointless tautology if the bread was an allegorical reference to the body of Christ in the Eucharist: some scholars imagine societies without material foundations, but Langland at least tried to resist this fantasy.

in his labour. Piers understands it as such and promises the knight that he will fulfil his own ploughman's work alongside "other laboures", so that the knight can carry out an idealized social role which should include just dealing with his tenants.[101] In this context it is undeniable that "teme" is taken in its most physically direct sense by all participants. With the understanding of the team of oxen here one can *contrast* exegetical commentaries like the following: "oxen used in ploughing, that is, discerning and spiritually perceiving the mysteries of the Scripture". Likewise the fourteenth-century bibliophile Richard of Bury writes of preachers as oxen ploughing in cultivation of the Lord's field.[102] In *Piers Plowman* itself we will arrive, after a long and winding path, at a point where, "Grace gave Piers a teme four gret oxen" and the team signifies the four evangelists (XIX.257–61). But in noticing this relationship we must not confuse the distant contexts: the relationship is emphatically not one of identity, in which the intervening Passus would be redundant. The two contexts are held apart, in tension.

In Passus VI Piers promises to "sowe" his "bredcorne" before he follows the way to Truth (VI.59–66), and he offers a bargain to the workers:

Who so helpeth me to eris or sowen here ar I wende,
Shal haue leue, bi owre lorde to lese here in heruest,
And make hem mery there-mydde maugre who-so bigrucceth it.
(VI.67–9)

The fruits of labour are an incentive to labour (VI.107–13). The contexts and the treatment of images of ploughing, harvest and merriment in this Passus should not be missed. Stephen Langton, we saw, assumed that as soon as the image of harvesters occurred it automatically signalled ("id est") doctors of theology, and undoubtedly harvesting images take on eschatological overtones—as in Matthew 13.39 Jesus says, "the harvest is the end of the world."[103] But Piers is not yet conscious of the religious potential of his images. Truly focusing the best aspirations of the pilgrims, he hopes to fulfil his social tasks and to have a merry harvest-time before he wends on his way, and he holds out this promise to the pilgrims. But Langland decides that such an orientation leads to disaster, which he depicts

---

[101] VI.22–58. See both P. M. Kean's articles on topics of justice in *RES*, 15 (1964), 241–61 and *Piers Plowman*, ed. Hussey, 76–110; for more realistic accounts of the situation see R. Hilton, *Bond Men Made Free* (London, 1973).

[102] Durandus, *Rationale*, I.3, tr. by J. M. Neale and B. Webb, *The Symbolism of Churches and Church Ornaments* (Leeds, 1843), 11; *Philobiblion*, IV. 91–5 quoted in another context by Robertson, *Preface*, 309.

[103] See Bloomfield, *Piers Plowman* (New Brunswick, 1961), 106–7, though he seems strangely to equate ploughing with harvesting.

with great energy (VI.117–30; 154–321). We will certainly misunderstand the poet's imagistic process if we reduce his writing at all points to the preacher's picturing models, ignoring his ability to create a context which strips the images of their allegorical dimensions and robs the reader of stock expectations. Furthermore we should note what qualities the dreamer-poet associates with Piers at this early stage of his own journey:

> Dame Worche-whan-tyme-is Pieres wyf dyȝte,
> His douȝter hiȝte Do-riȝte-so-or-thi-dame-shal-the-bete,
> His sone hiȝte Suffre-thi-souereynes-to-hauen-her-wille-
> Deme-hem-nouȝte-for-if-thow-doste-thow-shalt-it-dere-abugge.
>
> (VI.80–3)

The mode is similar to the one Piers uses in his description of the way to Truth in Passus V, and it makes the orientations of Piers clear enough. He is married, not mystically to God but to "Worche-whan-tyme-is", and his progeny are not the spiritual fruit of Christian salvation. Rather they imply the kind of outlook we have been tracing, one which relies totally on physical controls (VI.209; 175 ff.). Piers's own "douȝter" only does what is assumed to be "riȝte" for fear of chastisement from the labouring "wyf". Similarly, the "corne and catel", paid as "tythe", is robbed of the significances a different seed, harvest and animals have accrued by Passus XIX.

So by the time Piers resolves to be a pilgrim at the plough (V1.104), and he and his pilgrims "to the plow faren" (VI.107), the poet has evolved a context where such images are shorn of their habitual pious referents. The whole enterprise of ploughing and harvesting is kept to the imagistic status of, "Dikeres and delueres digged up balkes" (VI.109). This "reduction" works in precisely the way we saw Piers's role as ploughman, with its symbolic religious potential, being carefully "reduced" to that of a tinker's craft. To emphasise the control over the image, Langland tells us that Piers himself digs and tailors too (V.552), while in the tavern we meet a group which included:

> Watte the warner and his wyf bothe,
> Tymme the tynkere and tweyne of his prentis,
> Hikke the hakeneyman . . .
> . . .
> Dawe the dykere . . .
>
> (V.316–18; 320)

The "tynkere" and "dykere" exist in the same mode as the "Dikeres" of the half acre scene, and as the "other werkeman" who help Piers (VI.107–18). When we see,

> setten somme and songen atte nale,
> And hulpen erie his half-acre with 'how! trollilolli!'
> (VI.117–18)

then my reference to the mode of the tavern scene in Passus V gains further meaning. It should also be remarked that the tavern scene had preceded the pilgrims' resolve to go on pilgrimage to find truth. So when we read that some workers "to please Perkyn piked up the wedes" (VI.113), we need not rush off to the allegorical dictionary, from which I have already quoted, find weeds read as lust and avarice, and feed these glosses into Langland's own context. Nor will we simply equate this weeding with a very different part of the same poem where *Liberum Arbitrium*,

> hath the londe to ferme
> Vnder Piers the Plowman to pyken it and to weden it.
> (XVI.16–17)

For the dreamer's perspective has by then reached a stage very different to the present one, as the study of Passus XVI revealed. Here, in Passus VI, Langland controls the context to show the limitations of the participants' religious perception by depriving the agricultural imagery of its inherited pious connotations. In the poet's view such deprivation is part cause, part effect of the discord and individualistic materialism shown in Passus VI (117–321). The pilgrims' own guide reacts to this situation in tellingly materialistic and superficial ways.

Further examples show that this argument holds true for the rest of Passus VI. Piers threatens his "trollilolling", drinking ploughmen:

> But ʒe aris the rather and rape ʒow to worch,
> Shal no greyne that groweth glade ʒow at nede
> (VI.120–21)

Typical of exegetes, as soon as Langton saw the word for ears of corn in the Book of Ruth he understood, "that is the meaning of the Sacred Page". In Passus XIX Grace will give Piers, "greynes the cardynales vertues" (XIX.269). But neither Langton's nor Grace's grain or corn occurs to Piers, for at this stage he himself, the focus for the pilgrims' aspirations, has an orientation which excludes such further figurative resonance. The tenor of his threat is reflected when he admits to Hunger that it is only "for defaut of her fode this folke is at my wille". When we are aware of this delimiting, the wasters' benign hope becomes especially, and realistically, comic:

Ac we preye for ʒow Pieres and for ʒowre plow both,
That God of his grace ʒowre grayne multiplye
(VI.127–8)

The humour undermines Piers too, for the outlook is as much his as
the pilgrims'. Likewise, when Piers threatens that unless the labourers
work and drive Truth's "teme", they will have to eat barley bread
and drink of the brook, he is not drawing on the potential of the
image "teme" any more than the knight did earlier. Piers's view of
Truth's "teme" is certainly restricted. In a somewhat similar way he
offers some physical comfort to the crippled and blind without any
sense of needing to play the role of priest and preacher, purveyor of
"spiritual" help. (VI.138–40).

Another image whose existence in Passus VI we may contrast with
Passus XIX is that of making "morter" (VI.144). In Passus XIX Piers
asks Grace to help him build God's house and in the ensuing description Grace "made a morter and Mercy it hiʒte"; this mortar is
made from Christ's blood (XIX.319–21). But despite the poignant
reference at VI.210, Piers is here not much concerned with Grace or
the Cross, or even "holy writ", in contrast to the situation in Passus
XIX (316–30). His language and his present state screen off any
further suggestions the image could make, and he puts the mortar
here on a par with digging and delving or bearing "mukke a-feld" (VI.
141–4). (The field where the "mukke" is taken is obviously neither
simply equivalent to the field of Passus XIX nor to the readings for
"field" provided by the allegorical dictionary we glanced at.) Such
limitations must encourage the Wasters:

Of the flowre and of thi flessche fecche whan vs liketh
And make vs murie ther-myde maugre thi chekes!
(VI.159–60)

Piers's aspirations and energies in this section are directed into the
same material realm as the Wasters', representing the best Langland
can conceive coming from such a stance.

It is thus apt that the dreamer's vision shows Piers and Hunger
collaborating, men being controlled by the most basic needs. But
Piers's collaborator is no simple personification of "Famine". He
can appeal to Biblical notions about labour and vengeance, and how
man should feed himself "with his feythful laboure" (VI.214–54).
This is because he too is controlled by the context. He is the figure
of Hunger appearing in a vision where the search is for Truth and
where the protagonists have been instructed in the rudiments of
Christianity (for example, V.485–513). Furthermore, he is in colla-
boration with one who is "a gyde" to the pilgrims. It is not enough
merely to say with Frank that the "names" of personifications are

necessarily "all-important".[104] The writer may be much more concerned with context and shades of meaning than such a generalization allows. Although such concern may be unusual in medieval figurative writing, it is not my task to prove that Langland's poetry "represents nothing more nor less than the quintessence of English medieval preaching gathered up into a single metrical piece of unusual charm and vivacity", nor that *Piers Plowman* is like the homilies, just one of the "derivatives from the exegetical tradition".[105]

It is interesting that at this stage Piers has to ask advice of Hunger, whereas in Passus XVI he instructs Jesus (the "creatour wexe creature") on the same subject:

> "ʒet I prey ʒow", quod Pieres "*par charite*, and ʒe kunne
> Eny leef of lechecraft lere it me, my dere,
> For some of my seruauntz and my-self bothe
> Of al a wyke worche nouʒt so owre wombe aketh."
>
> (VI.255–7)

We have already discussed the passage in which Piers "lered hym [God incarnate] lechecrafte", but at the moment Piers focuses and embodies a vision which is preoccupied with productive labour and social organization. During Passus VI there is little thought of *Christus Medicus* or any diagnosis of a "sikeness to vs alle" which is called *sin* (V.490). Figurative potential is subdued at this stage, and it is fair to say that such consistent control of the figurative process is not only impressive but is central to the poem's total structure and Langland's meaning.

There are two more images at the close of Passus VI which are relevant to my argument. Piers tells Hunger that he has "a cartmere" with which he draws off dung in the draught. He hopes by Lamas time to have "hervest in my croft". Again we notice that in Passus XIX it is Grace who gives Piers "a carte hyʒte Cristendome" drawn by "caples . . . Contricioun and Confessioun", and that the harvest is to be taken, not into the "croft" of Passus VI but into a barn which Grace builds—"holicherche on Englisshe" (XIX.314–30). Having observed this, and knowing the normal religious implications of harvesting images, we must concentrate on the context of B VI, and understand how the poet has again carefully, and evocatively, prevented the full religious development of the vision's images. It is a vague realization of the deprivation which urges Piers and dreamer onwards in their exploration.

---

[104] "The Art of Reading Medieval Personification-Allegory", in *Interpretations of Piers Plowman*, ed. Vasta, 226.
[105] G. Owst, *Literature and Pulpit in Medieval England* (second edn, Oxford, 1961), 549 (a similar judgement by S. J. Kahrl, "Allegory in Practice", *M Phil*, 63 (1965–6), 110); Robertson and Huppé, *Piers Plowman*, 16.

Passus VII is the passus of the controversial Pardon scene. Since the current study is definitely not an attempt to write anything like an over-all interpretation of *Piers Plowman*, I shall only treat the Pardon from my present approach to Langland's imagistic modes and processes.

The imperative from Truth which opens Passus VII is conveyed in the agricultural imagery analysed above. This imperative not only requires Piers, "to taken his teme and tulyen the erthe", but also to "holde hym at home and eryen his leyes". Anyone who helps Piers in any way will partake of the Pardon that Truth "purchased" Piers (VII.1–8). From his first entry the ploughman appeared to the pilgrims and the dreamer as Truth's "folwar" who does what Truth orders (V.544–6). This fact was of course in no way denied by the preceding discussion of Passus VI, where I argued that Piers functions as focus for an orientation which is materially directed and anti-figurative, however desirous the participants are to follow the way to Truth. In the vision there was the possibility, we saw, that this was only a temporary preparation for the full undertaking of the pilgrimage to Truth. But now the poet-dreamer thinks Truth tells Piers to "holde hym at home", and "taken his teme and tulyen the erthe"; the Pardon which Piers originally planned to seek on Pilgrimage (VI.65–6) is now associated with staying at home to labour there. Burrow comments that these lines (VII.1–8) mean that "the pilgrimage is abandoned." But when he claims that "the pilgrimage is, in another sense, complete", because the object of the pilgrimage was to get Truth's Pardon, I cannot agree that this inference in "unavoidable".[106] We found, in fact, that Passus VI cannot even be read as the description of men on "the way" to Truth, let alone achieving the journey. Burrow is surely wrong to claim a part of the object of pilgrimage—pardon (VI.65–6)—as the whole. For the final aim of the pilgrimage is finding Truth (V.517–20; 539; 562; 568 ff.; VI.1; 6). The dramatic significance of Truth's imperative is in the manner in which it forces Piers and the dreamer back into the half acre and the imagistic modes we have discussed. The "way" Piers thought was the "heighe way", must be discovered "at home" (VI.4–6; VII.5). The postponed pilgrimage is certainly not "completed", but it cannot be undertaken away from the perplexities and failures of the half-acre scene, and all the limitations of perspective manifested there. Langland does not imagine that he can see the sun "in its idea".[107]

---

[106] Burrow, "The Action of Langland's Second Vision", here quoted from its reprint in *Style and Symbolism in Piers Plowman*, ed. R. J. Blanch (Knoxville, 1968), 218; lively discussion of the Pardon in Kirk, *Dream Thought of Piers Plowman*, 80–100.

[107] Wallace Stevens, "Notes Towards a Supreme Fiction" in *Collected Poems* (London, 1966), 381.

But why, it will be asked, does the poet write that Truth now "purchased hym a pardoun"? But the "why" of this is, I think, central to the *finale* of the Passus, with the confrontation of Piers and Priest, and the dreamer's own bewilderment at this vision's conclusion. At the moment let us compare this gift with one in Passus XIX, which is offered by Christ after his Resurrection:

> [Crist] ʒaf Pieres power and pardoun he graunted
> To alle manere men mercy and forʒyfnes,
> Hym myʒte men to assoille of alle manere synnes,
> In couenant that thei come and knowleche to paye,
> To Pieres pardon the Plowman *redde quod debes.*
> Thus hath Pieres powere be his pardoun payed
> To bynde and to vnbynde bothe here and elles-where,
> And assoille men of alle synnes saue of dette one.
>
> (XIX.178–85)

This gift precedes Piers's ploughing, sowing and harvesting in Passus XIX. So in Passus XIX the vision has attained a point where Christ's Incarnation, Resurrection and Victory have been perceived, and Piers has become the figurative lens through which Langland invites us to see their effects in history. There Piers's pardon, ploughing and power all flow from Christ's acts. The passage in Passus VII contrasts strongly with the later one, and this is bound up with the kind of contrast we established between the imagery of Passus VI, with its suppressed figurative possibilities, and that of Passus XIX. At the opening of Passus VII Truth's Pardon merely sends us back to the half acre and its images. But at this stage there is no elaboration as to *how* such activity as we saw in Passus VI can offer any way out of the impasse Langland's vision discovered in that mode of existence. Nor is the nature or content of the Pardon actually stated until the end of the Passus, although the vision unfolds a lengthy gloss on the "Pardoun" before that. The point cannot be argued here, but it seems that the gloss acts largely as an all too neat and evasive wish-fulfilment (for example, VII.18–38). It only appears helpful if we forget Passus VI and the situation which Langland depicted there. The Pardon mentioned at the opening of Passus VII is glibly accepted and glossed without any examination as to *how*, in Langland's Christian terms, fallen man (V–VI) can live in "sin" and yet be pardoned by *Truth*. Nor is it asked in what ways man's vision and its images might have to develop and change in order to perceive the nature of the Pardon or the way it could be efficacious for human kind. But Langland was too honest a thinker and a poet to shirk these problems. Hence, so it seems to me, the stark "witnesse of treuthe" which the Pardon of Piers actually contains (VII.111). How this "pardoun" from Truth is "no pardoun" (VII.112) and yet is part of the Athanasian Creed and in "witnesse of Treuthe", is a paradox which it will take the rest of the poem to resolve. And the resolution of all enigmas, in so far as they are resolved, will take place in the acts of Christ. This is high-lighted by Passus XIX.178–85. I quoted that passage not to read it into a separate context, but to encourage Langland's critics to have patience and to resist the temptation to snatch at significances not yet earned, or to read off simple answers to enigmas which the poet himself finds so complex that he can only unfold them across a long and diffuse poetic process. In Passus VII neither the guide of the pilgrims, nor the dreamer, nor the readers have come to the point where the figurative potential of the agricultural imagery has been revealed, nor the point where the paradox of this "pardoun" can be lived with. The irritation between Piers and the Priest, together with the dreamer's own dazed, unhappy and restless response to his vision's conclusion, surely witness the intense discomfort of having to live with unresolved and even, at this moment, not fully formu-lated and enigmatic paradoxes. The figurative poet who launches such a process, creates such stages, and faces them, is certainly rare. Piers responds to the priest's challenge by vowing:

"I shall cessen of my sowyng," quod Pieres, "and swink nouȝt so
　　harde,
Ne about my bely-ioye so bisi be namor!
Of preyers and of penaunce my plow shal ben hereafter
And wepen whan I shulde slepe though whete-bred me faille. . . . "
(VII.117–20)

The shock of having the Pardon "impugned" has for the first time forced the image of ploughing to take on a figurative aspect, for it has challenged the accepted perspective. It is certainly not yet the Christ-created figurative plough that is encountered in the visions we are following, but here there is a movement towards another kind of agriculture. The movement will finally gather momentum in the passage in Passus XVI which we have already examined; there it will be understood how the temporal dimension of history is necessary for the Christian's pilgrimage. Passus X. 456–84 tells us, "plowmen and pastoures and pore comune laboreres" will be saved, "for her pure byleue". This "pure byleue" is the heart and object of the pilgrimage. Piers himself is now in a position to be a different kind of "lens", for us and the dreamer, and his resolution confronts us dramatically with these new bearings.

Before discussing the agricultural imagery of Passus XIX, there are a few places *en route* which deserve some notice. In Passus XIII we meet Haukyn who seems to the dreamer to be "a mynstral"—"as me tho thouȝte"—and who is referred to as "the actyf man" (XIII.220ff.; XVI.2). Undeniably Haukyn's own vision sees Piers in the role we have just described in Passus VI.[108] Haukyn does not have any understanding of the figurative possibilities of his own language, and he plainly sees "Peres the Plowman" as separate from the prelatical order (XIII.234–7). So when Haukyn says that he is "Actyf" and produces "bred", "for alle trewe trauillours and tilieres of the erthe", we must not think that Haukyn has attained the figurative vision of Passus XIX, or even that he imagines a ploughing which can consist of "preyers and penaunce" (XIII.238–9; VII.119). Take Haukyn's cart and plough for instance: he boasts how when "no carte" came to London bearing his "wafres", there was "a carful commune" (XIII.264–8). This is no figurative cart, although potentially the image is capable of the extension—"A carte, hyȝte Cristendome to carye Pieres sheues" (XIX.327). But that "carte" will be created by Grace, not Haukyn, and is released through Christ's triumph. Later Haukyn confesses:

> ȝif I ȝede to the plow I pynched so narwe,
> That a fote-londe or a forwe fechen I wolde,
> Of my nexte neighboure nymen of his erthe;
> And if I rope, ouer-reche or ȝaf hem red that ropen
> To seise to me with her sykel that I ne sewe neure.
>
> (XIII.371–5)

The last offence is of course directly against the law of Deuteronomy 23.25. And whereas at XV.558 Anima will use this text figuratively (tropologically, in exegetical terminology), Haukyn's perspective has deprived this image, and the image of ploughing, of any deeper significance. To realize this, we have to be awake to the poet's delimiting context, and also to the process which will once more create the figurative resonance of the language as the vision's own perspective moves towards the Incarnation of Christ and the effects of his acts. Here there is no need to make detailed contrasts between Haukyn's use of these images and their use in Passus XIX, because the contrasts are akin to those made in examining Passus VI.

In Passus XIV Patience opposes Haukyn's one dimensional outlook:

> "And I shall purueye the paste," quod Pacyence, "though no plow erie,
> And floure to fede folke with as best be for the soule,
> Though neuere greyne growed ne grape vppon vyne."
>
> (XIV.28–30)

---

[108] See Stella Maguire, "The Significance of Haukyn, *Activa Vita*, in *Piers Plowman*", RES, 25 (1949), 97–109.

Here Patience deprives Haukyn of images he himself has robbed of religious possibilities. I exemplified exegetical readings of "plow" and "greyne", but in depriving man of basic images whose religious possibilities he is ignoring, Patience and the poet perhaps recommend St Augustine's advice, "descend, that ye may ascend, and ascend to God."[109] Langland wishes to purge Haukyn's images, and it should not, once again, be necessary to point out the comparisons with exegetes' "greyne" and "plow" or with those of Passus XIX.[110]

Agricultural imagery is used a little more fully in Passus XV. Anima criticizes the earthly priests who carry silver girdles, daggers and trinkets, and complains that even the "portous that shulde be his plow *placebo* to segge", is only used if crossed with silver (XV. 122). Here Anima employs the plough image just as Piers had done after the priest challenged him in Passus VII, although it is not developed and does not have the weight it will attain. Later in Passus XV Anima actually takes the image in a similar way to one of the readings we met in the thirteenth-century allegorical dictionary referred to earlier. The compiler wrote, "the field is the wild [inculta] heathen" and Anima tells the dreamer that "Hethene is to mene after hethe and untiled erthe" (XV.451). But the etymology comes in a piece of teaching about baptism and is again not developed. How could it be, when the dynamic which shows the creation of the means for cultivation has not yet been fully achieved and grasped in the vision?

We discussed, in detail, the way in which the tree of Charity's allegorical modes drive dreamer and reader towards the vision of *Christus Victor*.[111] Through Passus XVIII we follow the temporal revelation to its climax in hell. The focal symbol and saving agent visible in the dreamer's perception has at last coincided with Christ: Piers and Christ now *seem* indistinguishable to the visionary, for the Incarnate Christ is now "seen" through Piers (e.g. XVIII.10–35; XIX.5–14). The "sikeness to us alle" has been attacked by, "I, that am lorde of lyf", and he that is "doctour of deth" has been bound with chains. All the four daughters of God are reconciled, and the poet's vision has now seen Time "run back, and fetch the age of gold". The visionary's waking response is a magnificent testimony of the nature and power that the vision and language have generated:

Tyl the daye dawed this damaiseles daunced,
That men rongen to the resurrexioun and riȝt with that I waked,
And called Kitte my wyf and Kalote my dauȝter—

---

[109] *Confessions*, IV.19, tr. E. B. Pusey (Collier Books edn), 58.
[110] See also XIV.67; XV.105.
[111] On this Christ, see G. Aulen, *Christus Victor*, tr. A. G. Hebert (London, 1953) and Bloomfield, *Piers Plowman*, 125.

"Ariseth and reuerenceth goddes resurrexioun,
And crepeth to the crosse on knees . . ."
(XVIII.424–8)[112]

Yet at this point some critics consider Langland's mode to be that of the exegetes or preachers we studied previously:

What then can Will's married state imply but that he has ceased . . . to be a hermit? . . . as a faculty, the will is united with memory and intellect in the image of God. He is truly married; that is he is at one with memory and intellect in the celebration of the Cross. . . . From the union of himself and intellect comes the contemplative *memoria* and all three are as one directed toward charity.[113]

Passages from St Bernard and Raban Maur are taken as sufficient exegesis of the poet's lines. The scholars also assume that this exegesis justifies them in reading "memory" and "intellect" for the poet's "Kitte my wyf and Kalote my dauȝter".[114] I mention their interpretation because it exemplifies the confusion of different modes which is one of the prevalent tendencies in work on medieval figurative writing. For this reason it is worth pursuing, although it has nothing to do with the agricultural imagery of Passus XIX.

Langland himself, as we saw, does employ picture models, but these are usually placed at a point in the total process which gives their use some particular meaning. They have to be passed through, and the poet implies, "that was a way of putting it—not very satisfactory."[115] An obvious example is the friar's attempt to resolve the dreamer's doubts about salvation when all are fallen ("*sepcies in die cadit iustus*", VIII.21). The friar gives an extended picture model, preacher as he is, and extracts an answer; but the dreamer, intelligently, finds it actually solves nothing (VIII.57–8). Another clear case, discussed earlier in this chapter, was Anima's allegorical tree imagery in Passus XVI, and there we saw how it stood in a special relation to the developing context. If the poet integrates this kind of writing into a search which passes on to other modes, it is certainly bad reading to turn all parts of his process into picture models; the picture models he does present only gain interest and meaning from

---

[112] On the tradition of these dancing ladies, H. Travers, *The Four Daughters of God* (Bryn Mawr, 1907) and his article in *PMLA*, 40 (1925), 44–92.
[113] Robertson and Huppé, *Piers Plowman*, 204–5.
[114] The scholars quote and cite Bernard, *P. Lat.* 184. 546–7, Rabanus, *P. Lat.* 110.84.
[115] T. S. Eliot, *East Coker*, 68; relevant here are my previous comments on Passus V.568–613 and on Anima's exegesis in Passus XVI; similar examples VIII.27–56; XIII.119–22; IX. 1–24, 48–9; XVII.315–48; V.136–42 (but notice its relation to Anima's exegesis in XVI); VI.83–3; XIII.37–62, where the mode is in startling contrast to the other menu.

their participation in the dreamer's mental evolution embodied in the poet's own particular process. At the risk of labouring the point, we can look at another passage where Langland employs a mode akin to the one which Robertson and Huppé find at Passus XVIII.425–8. In Passus XIII, "Haukyn the actyf man" is shown to have "ysoiled his cote" (XIII.458). The coat is labelled, "cote of Crystendome as holy kirke bileueth", and the things that have soiled it are, "Pruyde ... vnboxome speche", and so on—the seven sins and variations thereon (XIII.272–460). Conscience then promises to teach Haukyn to "clawe thi cote of alkynnes filthe/*Cordis contricio*", to wash and wring it, with *confessio*, and sew it up with *satisfaccio* (XIV.16–21). Now into this picture model (though it is more fluid and locally evoked than most picture models I have discussed), the poet introduces "an houswyf, hewen and children" for Haukyn, and at once adds the gloss: "*Vxorem duxy et ideo non possum venire*" (XIV.3). What has Haukyn not been able to come to? Luke 14.12–24 is the text the poet alludes to, for his quotation is from Luke 14.20. He has been unable to attend the Lord's feast. Now the nature of the model which uses this allusion, and the fact that the object of "cannot come" is explicitly in Luke's text and not in Passus XIV, seems to demand that we treat Haukyn's "houswyf" as part of the model alongside the children and possessions. We will be justified in supposing that the way medieval readers of Luke 14.12–24 understood the text of verse twenty will be relevant to the poet's picturing model. Robertson and Huppé have given ample evidence that the excuses in Luke's parable were read as signifying, "love for terrestrial goods ... attractions of the senses ... the pleasures of the flesh". These prevented men from "a true marriage with Christ".[116] That a wife can indeed bear this kind of significance in Langland's own picture models can be confirmed internally (though Robertson and Huppé do not bother with this). In Passus XVII, the Samaritan gives the dreamer a picture model based on things which drive men from their houses. One of these is the contentious wife of Proverbs 19.13. From this he deduces, "the wyf is owre wikked flesshe that wil nouȝt be chasted", and develops the reading (XVII.317–32). There is no doubt that Langland is using the kind of picture model we have met so frequently. When Haukyn, returning to Passus XIV, has received instructions in the three parts of penance (read off the picture model), Conscience promises that if he follows the teaching then shall

> no mynstral be more worth amonges pore and riche,
> Than Haukynnes wyf the wafrere with his *actiua-vita*.
>
> (XIV.26–7)

---

[116] *Piers Plowman*, 169–70.

These two lines made Donaldson comment, "the sudden mention of
Haukyn's wife is odd. Is Haukyn being so generalized as to compre-
hend the female representatives of the active life?"[117] However, we
now see that the "mention of Haukyn's wife" is actually not all that
sudden. Although Robertson and Huppé say the lines signify that
"through his influence his wife will become a good ministrel", the
picture model probably requires us to read "flesshe" from "haukyn-
nes wyf"— for after his penance it would be orthodox enough to
believe that his flesh (the female principle) will be well and valuably
married to his true self (the male principle, which was taken as the
reason).[118] Clumsy and unattractive as the approach is, it seems to be
demanded by the poet's figurative mode at *that* point. However, like
the other picture models in the poem it is fortunately neither
definitive nor final, a stage through which we pass. The difference
between such picture models and the context and mode of the
passage from which the comparative analysis began (XVIII.424–8)
should be quite clear by now. The passage in Passus XVIII is, in
fact, part and product of an extremely personalized "disclosure
model", and we must avoid confusions of modes and contexts which
would dissolve the poet's own figurative dynamic, turning the poem
into a wasteland of bygone mediocrity.

In Passus XIX and XX Langland is concerned to explore the means
by which Christ's acts can still be efficacious in the present, and the
way the present responds to such means. Christ's acts have brought
the spirit into the letter and the allegorical development of agricultural imagery is now based on the transforming power of *Christus
Victor*.[119] The time which Jesus foretold is now considered: "it is
expedient to you that I go: for if I go not, the Paraclete will not come
to you; but if I go, I will send him to you" (John 16.7). Christ
disappears from the dreamer's (and reader's) field of vision (XIX.
186–7), and Piers now becomes the lens through which present
effects of Christ's acts and his Spirit are focused.[120] After an insight
into the Pentecostal descent, when those in time present seem to
participate with those in time past who first experienced the *spiritus
paraclitus* (XIX.196–207), the dreamer finds that, "thanne bigan
Grace to go with Piers Plowman" (XIX.208). Christ himself, after
his triumph over Death and Hell, had given Piers "power and
pardoun", but now we are to watch *how* this can be.

Grace, who follows the Ascension of Christ, declares:

> My prowor and my plowman Piers shal ben on erthe,
> And for to tulye treuthe a teme shal he haue.
>
> (XIX.255–6)

---

117 Donaldson, *Piers Plowman*, 141 n. 3.
118 Robertson and Huppé, *Piers Plowman*, 171.
119 *Exégèse*, I.1. chapter V; I.2.439 ff. and chapter VIII. II. chapter II.
120 Compare XIX.195–201, and Acts 2.1–4.

He does not refer us back to the dreamer's perception of Piers in Passus V to VII, but, in the time-scheme of the vision, sees Grace making provision for the future. We did not find such oxen in any "teme" of Passus V to VII:

> Grace gaue Piers a teme foure gret oxen;
> That on was Luke, a large beste and a lowe-chered,
> And Marke, and Mathew the thrydde myghty bestes bothe,
> And Ioigned to hem one Iohan most gentil of alle,
> They prys nete of Piers plow passyng alle other.
>
> (XIX.257–61)

The availability of the great oxen has only been fully realized through the processes leading up to this post-Pentecostal stage. After the ploughing there is the harrowing. The harrow-drawers are "foure stottis", Augustine, Ambrose, Gregory and Jerome. On the two harrows, the poet comments in a form we have met so often: "*Id est, vetus testamentum et nouum*" (XIX.268). Both the "greynes" of Passus VI and those in Langton's exegesis of the Book of Ruth have been mentioned; here are Grace's:

> And Grace gaue greynes the cardynales vertues
> And sewe hem in mennes soule . . .
>
> (XIX.269–70)

To Langton, the grains were the *sententiae* of Scripture; to the poet they are now "cardynales vertues", but the mode will seem similar. There is no need to follow these seventy-three lines of agricultural imagery in detail because Langland's mode here continues as in the two passages just quoted. The seeds are read as ethical qualities, the harrow, "wyth olde lawe and newe lawe", prepares the ground, "mannes soule", for the growth of love. Then we come to the barn of Unity, a typical medieval figurative edifice.[121] Ethical and doctrinal statements are read off its various parts, and taken in isolation, the only unusual feature of the edifice is Langland's brevity.

Elizabeth Salter and Derek Pearsall classified the scene fairly enough, as "diagrammatic Allegory", commenting that it "only barely achieves any sort of dramatic presence—in contrast to an earlier ploughing scene".[122] I have shown how the passage contrasts and *had* to contrast with the "ploughing scene" of Passus VI. Taken on its own it resembles any simplistic orthodox picture model, but

---

[121] On these see R. D. Cornelius, *The Figurative Castle* (Bryn Mawr, 1930); *Exégèse*, 2.41–60; Katzenellenbogen, *Allegories of the Virtues and Vices*, 43 ff.; some examples in chapter three of the present book.

[122] *Piers Plowman*, ed. Salter and Pearsall, 16; see pp. 13–16.

read in its total context is supersedes this limitation. We are aware
that behind the "diagrammatic allegory" lies a great area of related
imagery, focusing various stages of the dreamer's mental and
historical pilgrimage. In Langland's organization, imagery which had
been deprived of its figurative potential has been realigned through
the "spirit"-bringing acts of Christ. Although the poet is using the
inherited techniques of picturing models at this point, both models
and readings grow out of a multi-dimensional process. Though the
figurative "spirit" of Christian dispensation is now revealed to the
dreamer, there are still widespread continuities with the world of
Passus V–VII:

> Pieres the Plowman peyneth hym to tulye
> As wel for a wastour and wenches of the stuwes,
> As for hym-self and his servauntz . . .
>
> (XIX.434–6; see 424 ff.)

The allegorical structure declares the Christian claim that if the old
crop is to be saved (Passus VI, XVI, XIX) it is through God's acts
in human history and society. If *Piers Plowman* has important affini-
ties with exegesis they are here, with central aspects of its theology,
for we recall how the theory of exegesis maintains that Christ's acts
both create and reveal the figurative dimension (the "spirit") of pre-
Incarnation imagery and events. In the area of agricultural imagery
which we have been studying, the poem's dynamic exploits this
conception, adapted to express the confusion, frustration, development and insights of a fourteenth-century man, the poet's dreamer.
The passage in the final Passus (XX.50–6) where the dreamer falls
asleep is a finely organized return to the situation of time present
without losing the newly won perspective:

> anon I felle aslepe,
> And mette ful merueillously that, in mannes forme,
> Antecryst cam thanne and alle the croppe of treuthe
> Torned it vp so doune and ouertilte the rote,
> And made fals sprynge and sprede and spede mennes nedes;
> And eche a contre ther he cam he cutte awey treuthe,
> And gert gyle growe there as he a god were.

Antichrist's activities are thus imagistically connected with those of
the "Fende" seen in an earlier vision. There he tried to destroy the
fruit of the tree grown "thorw god and thorw good men", shook the
root, laid a ladder against the tree and prevented its development
(XVI.940–5). Antichrist's success is inevitable in a society lacking
what Blake called "the Divine Vision". Langland's scene depicts this
situation, and the fact that he does so in such a different way from

the earlier Passus (V–VII) reflects the evolution of perception through the dreamer's journey: the "croppe of trouthe" so vital in Passus XIX and XX is not the crop of the half acre in Passus VI, but it is imagistically and conceptually related in ways I have discussed. Piers has been the saving agent envisaged by men's aspirations, in him the dreamer and others symbolize the saving power imagined and conceived at particular stages of the pilgrimage.[123] No ending could be better integrated to the total movement of Langland's poem than the resolve amidst the social discord and individual bafflement of time present "to seke Piers the Plowman", the figure who embodies "the Divine Vision in time of trouble" (*Jerusalem*, 95).

---

[123] I should perhaps remark here that I have found no need to discard my "working hypothesis" for following the function of Piers in the poem. Whatever other readers decide about its use no interpretation of Piers can afford to treat this symbolic figure as a naive picture model, extracting a series of dogmatic propositions. He is a focal figure in a visionary process and he became an essential part of Langland's own thinking and his attempt to resolve his, and his society's confusions.

Select Bibliography

They are not alwaies the Best men that blot most paper; Truth is not, I fear, so Voluminous, nor swells into such a mighty bulk as our Books doe.

John Smith

Because the footnotes provide adequate reference to materials used in writing this book, as well as to more relevant scholarship, this Bibliography is highly selective: it is intended as a guideline to only the most central materials I have used, and in the case of section C as encouragement to students to study the social and intellectual context within which Langland was struggling to grasp "the way", and out of which *Piers Ploughman* emerged. This section suggests the area where, it seems to me, the most necessary and potentially fruitful work on Langland (and, indeed, the literature of his period) is yet to be done.

A Chief primary material

1 *Exegetical and theological*

A Middle English Treatise on Hermeneutics, ed. R. H. Bowers. PMLA, 65 (1950), 590–600

Augustine, *Against Lying*, in *Seventeen Short Treatises of St Augustine*, tr. by members of the English Church (Oxford, 1847)

Augustine, *On Christian Doctrine*, tr. D. W. Robertson (Indianapolis, 1958)

Augustine, *The City of God*, tr. M. Dods (New York, 1950)

Augustine, *The Trinity*, tr. S. MacKenna (Washington, 1963)

Dionysius the Areopagite (pseudo-Dionysius). *Dionysius the Areopagite on the Divine Names and the Mystical Theology*, tr. C. E. Rolt (London, second edn., 1966)

Denis the Carthusian, *Dionysii Carthusiani Enarrationes piae ac eruditae*. 8 vols (Cologne, 1531–5)

Glossa Ordinaria. See Nicholas of Lyra; also in *P. Lat.*, 113–14

Henricus Totting de Oyta, *Quaestio de Sacra Scriptura*, ed. A. Lang (Munich, 1932)

Holcot, Robert, *In Librum Sapientiae Salomonis Praelectiones CCXIII* (Basle, 1586)

Hugh of St Victor, *The Didascalicon*, tr. J. Taylor (New York, 1961)

Nicholas of Lyra, *Postillae* (*Textus bibliae cum Glossa ordinaria, Nicholai de Lyra postilla, Moralitatibus eiusdem, Pauli Burgensis, AdditionibusMatthiae Thoring Replicis*). 6 vols (Basle, 1506–8)

Origen, *Against Celsus*, tr. H. Chadwick (Cambridge, 1965)

Plotinus, *The Enneads*, tr. S. MacKenna, fourth edition revised by B. S. Page (London, 1969)

Thomas Aquinas, *Summa Theologiae*. Latin text and English translation, by the Dominicans from the English speaking Provinces (London, 1963 ff.)

2 *Poets, poetics, preachers*

The Abbey of the Holy Ghost, ed. G. G. Perry, in EETS, o.s., 26, 1867 (revised 1913)

Boccaccio, Giovanni, *On Poetry, Being the Preface and the Fourteenth and Fifteenth Books of Boccaccio's Genealogia Deorum Gentilium*, tr. C. G. Osgood (Princeton, 1930)

Castel of Love, ed. C. Horstmann, in *Minor Poems of the Vernon MS*, EETS, o.s., 98, 1892

Dante, *The Divine Comedy*, Italian text with tr. by J. D. Sinclair. 3 vols (revised edn., London, 1971)

Dante, *Dantis Alagherii Epistolae*, ed. and tr. P. Toynbee, (Oxford, 1920)

Deguileville, Guillaume de, *Pèlerinage d l'Ame*, ed. J. Stürzinger (London, 1895)

Deguileville, Guillaume de, *Pèlerinage de la vie humaine*, ed. J. Stürzinger (London, 1893)

Deguileville, Guillaume de, [*Lydgate's*] *De Guilleville's Pilgrimage of the Life of Man*, ed. F. J. Furnival. EETS, e.s., 77, 83, 92, 1899–1904

The Epistle of Othea, Translated from the French text of Christine de Pisan by Stephen Scrope, ed. C. F. Bühler. EETS, o.s., 264, 1970

Gerson, Jean, *Six Sermons Français Inédits*, ed. L. Mourin (Paris, 1946)

Gesta Romanorum, ed. S. J. Herrtage. EETS, e.s., 33, 1879

Henry of Lancaster, *Le Livre de Seyntz Medicines*, ed. E. J. Arnold (Oxford, 1940)

Kleiner mittelenglische texte ed. M. Foster. Anglia, 30 (1918), 152–4.

Langland, William, *The Vision of William Concerning Piers the Plowman in three parallel texts together with Richard the Redeless*, ed. W. W. Skeat. 1886 (London, 1968)

Lydgate, John, *The Life of Our Lady*, ed. J. Lauritis et al. (Pittsburgh, 1961)

Lydgate, John, *The Minor Poems*, ed. H. N. MacCracken. EETS, e.s., 107, 1910 and o.s., 192, 1933

Mirk's Festial, ed. T. Erbe. EETS, e.s., 96, 1905

The Mirroure of Mannes Saluacion, edited for the Roxburghe Club (London, 1888)

Three Middle English Sermons from the Worcester Chapter Manuscript F.10. ed. D.M. Grisdale (Kendal, 1939)

B Chief secondary works

1 Exegesis and theology

Barr, J., *Old and New in Interpretation* (London, 1966)

Bruyne, E. de, *Études Médiévale Esthétique*. 3 vols (Brussels, 1946)

Charity, A. C., *Events and their Afterlife: The Dialectics of Christian Typology in the Bible and Dante* (Cambridge, 1966)

Chenu, M-D., "Involucrum: Le Mythe selon les théologiens médiévaux", AHDLMA, 22 (1955), 75–9

Chenu, M-D., "Les deux âges de l'allégorisme scripturaire au moyen âge", RTAM, 18 (1951), 19–28

Chenu, M-D., "Histoire et Allégorie au douzième siècle, in *Fesgabe Joseph Lortz*, vol. 2 (Baden-Baden, 1958)

Chenu, M-D., "Théologie Symbolique et Exégèse Scolastique aux XIIIe–XIIIe siècles", in *Mélanges J. de Ghellinck* (Gembloux, 1951)

Chydenius, J., "The Theory of Medieval Symbolism", CHL, 27 (1960), 1–42

Daniélou, J., *From Shadows to Reality*, tr. W. Hibberd (London, 1960)

Daniélou, J., *Origen*, tr. W. Mitchell (London, 1955)

Gilson, E., "Michel Menot et la technique du sermon médiéval", *Revue d'Histoire Franciscaine*, 2 (1925), 299–350

Hanson, R. P. C., *Allegory and Event* (London, 1959)

Klibansky, R., *The Continuity of the Platonic Tradition in the Middle Ages* (London, 1939)

Lampe, G. W. H. and Woolcombe, K. J., *Essays in Typology* (London, 1957)

Lubac, H. de, "À Propos de l'Allégorie Chrétienne", RSR, 47 (1959), 5–43

Lubac, H. de, *Exégèse Médiévale: Les Quatre Sens De L'Écriture*. 4 vols (Paris, 1959–63).

Lubac, H. de, *Histoire et Esprit: L'intelligence de l'Écriture d'après Origène* (Paris, 1950)

Lubac, H. de, "'Typologie' et 'Allégorisme'", RSR, 34 (1947), 180–226

Nineham, D. E., ed. *The Church's Use of the Bible Past and Present* (London, 1963)

Owst, G., *Literature and Pulpit in Medieval England* (second edn., Oxford, 1961)

Pépin, J., "S. Augustin et la fonction protreptique de l'allégorie", *Recherches Augustiniennes* 1 (1958), 243–86

Pépin, J., *Mythe et Allégorie*, (Paris, 1958)

Pontet, M., *L'Exégèse de St Augustin Predicateur* (Paris, 1946)

Ramsey, I. T., *Christian Discourse* (London, 1965)

Ramsey, I. T., *Models and Mystery* (London, 1964)

Ramsey, I. T., *Religious Language* (London, 1957)

Reeves, M., *The Influence of Prophecy in the Later Middle Ages* (London, 1969)

Smalley, Beryl, "The Bible and Eternity: John Wyclif's Dilemma", *JWCI*, 27 (1964), 73–89

Smalley, Beryl, *English Friars and Antiquity in the Early Fourteenth Century* (Oxford, 1960)

Smalley, Beryl, "John Wyclif's *Postilla Super Totam Bibliam*", *Bodleian Library Record*, 4 (1953), 185–205.

Smalley, Beryl, "Problems of Exegesis in the Fourteenth Century", *Miscellanea Medievalia*, 1 (1962), 266–74

Smalley, Beryl, *The Study of the Bible in the Middle Ages*. Revised edition (1952) (Indiana, 1964)

Spicq, C., *Esquisse d'une Histoire de l'Exégèse Latine au Moyen Age* (Paris, 1944)

Spicq, C., "Pourquoi le Moyen Age n'a-t-il pas davantage pratiqué l'exégèse littérale?" *Les Sciences Philosophiques et Théologiques*, 1 (1941–2), 169–78

2 *Criticism*

Auerbach, E., "Figura", pp. 11–71 in his *Scenes from the Drama of European Literature*, tr. R. Manheim (New York, 1959)

Auerbach, E., "Typological Symbolism in Medieval Literature", *Yale French Review*, 9 (1952), 3–10

Bethurum, D., ed. *Critical Approaches to Medieval Literature. Selected Papers from the English Institute, 1958–9* (New York, 1960)

Bloomfield, M. W., *Piers Plowman as a Fourteenth-Century Apocalypse* (New Brunswick, 1961)

Bloomfield, M. W., "Symbolism in Medieval Literature", *MPhil*, 56 (1958), 73–81

Donahue, C., "Patristic Exegesis in the Criticism of Medieval Literature: The Summation", in Bethurum, *Critical Approaches*, pp. 61–82

Donaldson, E. T., "Patristic Exegesis in the Criticism of Medieval Literature: The Opposition", in Bethurum, *Critical Approaches*, pp. 1–26

Donaldson, E. T., *Piers Plowman. The C-Text and Its Poet. 1949* (London, 1966)

Dunning, T. P., "The Structure of the B-Text of *Piers Plowman*", *RES*, 7 (1956), 225–37

Frank R. W., "The Art of Reading Medieval Personification-Allegory", *ELH*, 20 (1953), 237–50

Frank, R. W., *Piers Plowman and the Scheme of Salvation* (New Haven, 1953)

Feeman, M. B., "The Iconography of the Merode Altarpiece", *Metropolitan Bulletin of Art*, 16 (1957), 130–9

Hussey, S. S., ed. *Piers Plowman: Critical Approaches* (London, 1969)

Kaske, R. E., "Chaucer and Medieval Allegory", *ELH*, 30 (1963), 175–92

Kaske, R. E., "Patristic Exegesis in the Criticism of Medieval Literature: The Defence", in Bethurum, *Critical Approaches*, pp. 27–60

Kirk, E., *The Dream Thought of Piers Plowman* (New Haven, 1972)

Mazzeo, J., "Dante's Conception of Poetic Expression", *RR*, 47 (1956), 241–58

Mazzeo, J., "Dante and the Pauline Modes of Vision", *HTR*, 50 (1957), 275–306

Panofsky, E. and Saxl, F., "Classical Mythology in Medieval Art", *Metropolitan Museum Studies*, 4 (1923–3), 228–80

Robertson, D. W., "The Doctrine of Charity in Medieval Literary Gardens: A Topical Approach through Symbolism and Allegory", *Spec*, 26 (1951), 24–49

Robertson, D. W., *A Preface to Chaucer. Studies in Medieval Perspectives* (Princeton, 1963)

Robertson, D. W. and Huppé, B. F., *Piers Plowman and Scriptural Tradition* (Princeton, 1951)

Salter, Elizabeth, "Medieval Poetry and the Figural View of Reality", *PBA*, 54 (1968), 73–92

Salter, Elizabeth, *Piers Plowman: An Introduction* (Oxford, 1962)

Singleton, C. S., "Dante's Allegory", *Spec*, 25 (1950), 78–86

Smith, B., *Traditional Imagery of Charity in Piers Plowman* (The Hague, 1966)

Vasta, E., ed. *Interpretations of Piers Plowman* (Notre Dame, 1968)

Zeeman [Salter], Elizabeth, "Piers Plowman and the Pilgrimage to Truth", *ES*, II (1958), 1–16

C Guidelines towards an attempt to grasp the social totality within which Langland's poem is written, and within which it must be interpreted

1 *Primary materials, besides those in A(2)*

The Book of the Knight of the Tower, tr. W. Caxton, ed. M. Y. Offord, *EETS*, s.s., 1971

Chaucer, Geoffrey, *The Works*, ed. F. N. Robinson (second edn., Repr., London, 1968)

Dobson, R. B., ed *The Peasants Revolt of 1381* (London, 1970)

Fasciculi Zizanorum Magistri Johannis Wyclif cum tritico, ed. W. W. Shirley. Rolls Series, 1858

Gower, John, *The Complete Works*, ed. G. C. Macaulay. 4 vols (Oxford, 1899–1902)

Gower, John, *The Major Latin Works*, tr. E. W. Stockton (Seattle, 1962)

Julian of Norwich, *Revelations of Divine Love*, ed. G. Warwick (thirteenth edn., London, 1949)

Margery Kempe, *The Book of Margery Kempe*, ed. S. B. Meech and H. E. Allen. EETS, o.s., 212, 1940

Myers, A. R., ed. *English Historical Documents*, IV, 1327–1485 (London, 1969)

Pearl, ed. E. V. Gordon (London, 1953)

Robbins, R. H., ed. *Historical Poems of the XIVth and XVth Centuries* (New York, 1959)

Upland, Jack. *Jack Upland, Friar Daw's Reply and Upland's Rejoinder*, ed. P. L. Heyworth (London, 1968)

Wyclif, John. *De Ecclesia*, ed. I. Loserth (London, 1886)

2 *Secondary material*

Bloch, M., *Feudal Society*, tr. L. A. Manyon (second edn., London, 1962)

Duby, G., *Rural Economy and Country Life in the Medieval West*, tr. C. Postan (London, 1968)

Hilton, R., *Bond Men Made Free. Medieval Peasant Movements and the English Uprising of 1381* (London, 1973)

Hilton, R., *The Decline of Serfdom in Medieval England* (London, 1969)

Hilton, R., *The Economic Development of Some Leicestershire Estates in the Fourteenth and Fifteenth Centuries* (Oxford, 1947)

Holmes, G. A., *The Estates of the Higher Nobility in Fourteenth Century England* (Cambridge, 1957)

Kosminsky, E. A., *Studies in the Agrarian History of England in the Thirteenth Century* (Oxford, 1956)

Kosminsky, E. A., "Feudal Rent in England", *Past and Present*, 7 (1955)

Leff, G., *Bradwardine and the Pelagians* (Cambridge, 1957)

Leff, G., *Heresy in the Later Middle Ages*. 2 vols (Manchester, 1967)

Manning, B. L., *The People's Faith in the Time of Wyclif* (Cambridge, 1917)

Marx, K., *Pre-capitalist Economic Formations*, tr. J. Cohen, intr. E. J. Hobsbawm (London, 1964)

McFarlane, K. B., *Lancastrian Kings and Lollard Knights* (London, 1972)

MacFarlane, K. B., *The Nobility of Later Medieval England* (London, 1973)

Oberman, H. A., *The Harvest of Medieval Theology* (Cambridge, Mass., 1963)

Pantin, W. A., *The English Church in the Fourteenth Century* (Cambridge, 1955)

Postan, M. M., *Essays on Medieval Agriculture and General Problems of the Economy* (Cambridge, 1973)

Postan, M. M., *The Medieval Economy and Society* (London, 1972)

Power, E., *Medieval English Wool Trade* (London, 1941)

Tuck, A., *Richard II and the English Nobility* (London, 1973)

Ziegler, P., *The Black Death* (London, 1969)

Index

Agricultural imagery 73, 89–107, 109–25, 128–31
Allegory *passim*
  as process, 59–70, 71–131
Allen, J. B. 2n, 27n
Antichrist 130
Auerbach, E. 17, 20–23, 36
Augustine 16–17, 25–6, 28, 48n, 53–4, 57n, 62, 63, 69–70, 78n, 85, 91n, 96n, 125
Aulen, G. 125n
Ayers, R. W. 49–50

Barr, J. 10n
Bede 110
Bernard 19n, 62
Bible Examples of exegetical reading, 16–17, 20–26, 28–9, 28–9, 29–34, 37–8, 39–41, 53–4, 112
Bishop, I. 10–11
Black, M. 13n, 59–60
Blake, W. 1, 14, 15, 70, 71, 78, 130, 131
Bloomfield, M. W. 8–9, 18–19, 29, 64n, 77, 82n, 101n, 116n, 125n
Boccaccio 10–12, 55–7, 62
Boethius 78n
Boman, T. 10n
Bonsirven, J. 10n
Book of Vices and Virtues 112n
Bowers, R. H. 28n
Bruyne, E. de 19n
Burrow, J. 115n, 121

Carnegy, F. 77
Cassirer, E. 59
Charity, A. C. 10, 60n, 61n
Chaucer 35–6, 52
Chenu, M-D. 16
Christ 4, 21–6, 29–30, 34–8, 41–2, 47–9, 51, 58, 61, 63, 65–6, 68, 71–131
Chydenius, J. 19n, 59n
Coleridge, S. T. 14, 37–8, 52, 55n, 70, 88n
Collingwood, R. G. 50
Cornelius, R. D. 37n, 129n
Creator 65–7, 107
Curtius, E. 53n

Daniélou, J. 4n, 9–10, 20–22
Dante 11–12, 60–63, 64, 65, 68, 69, 75
Deguileville, Guillaume de 42–9, 102–3
Descroche, H. 17n
Dionysius the Areopagite 19n, 78
Dionysius the Carthusian 22–3, 24, 28–31, 32n
Donahue, C. 6–8, 17, 25, 36
Donaldson, E. T. 67n, 75–6, 79–81, 83, 86, 90–91, 93n, 97, 99, 110n, 128
Dunning, T. P. 7, 77, 114, 115n

Eden 29–31, 73
Eschatology 75
Euhemerism 11

Exegesis *passim*, 112–14, 130
   See also Bible

Fall 29–31, 47–9, 73, 84n, 96, 101–5
Fowler, D. C. 72–3, 84n
Frank, R. W. 74–5, 81–2, 83, 93n, 111, 114, 119–20
Fruit and chaf 52–70 *passim*

Gerson, Jean 39–40, 44
Gesta Romanorum 41n
Glossa 22, 24, 28
Goldmann, L. 108n
Gombrich, E. H. 41
Green, R. H. 11–12
Greenhill, E. S. 47–9
Gregory the Great 24, 110

Hanson, R. P. C. 9–10, 18, 34, 55n
Hawes, Stephen 42, 59
Henry of Lancaster 40–41, 44
Henryson, Robert 59
Hilton, R. 28n, 116n
History 1–50 *passim*, 34, 41, 48–51, 57–8, 63, 71–131 *passim*
Holcot, Robert 27, 86–7, 97n
Homily and allegory 33–51 *passim*, 64, 69, 71, 72, 86–7, 89, 109, 112–13, 117, 120, 126
Hugh of St Victor 19n
Huizinga, J. 67n
Huppé, B. F. 34n, 35–6, 71–2
   See also Robertson, D. W.

Incarnation 4, 19, 24, 37, 47–9, 51, 73, 93, 95, 107–9, 125
Irenaeus 20–21

Jacques de Vitry 112
Jeanroy, A. 48n
Jesse tree 83
Jones, H. S. V. 64n

Josipovici, G. 18n
Julian of Norwich 78

Kahrl, S. J. 120n
Kaske, R. E. 6, 84n, 86, 107, 108
Kelly, J. N. D. 16
Kirk, E. 64n, 76n, 84n, 86n, 111n, 121n
Kolve, V. A. 67n

Ladner, G. B. 69n
Lampe, G. W. H. 17
Langland, William *See Piers Plowman*
Langton, Stephen 112, 118, 129
Lawlor, J. 74–5
Leff, G. 28n

Moralizing allegory 17, 33–51 *passim*

Nature (and History) 18–19, 28
Nicholas of Lyra 22–3, 31–2, 34n, 60
Nuttall, A. D. 60n

Ong, W. J. 53n
Origen 9–10, 16, 17–18, 21–2, 23, 34, 58
Owst, G. 120

Pantin, W. A. 112n
Pascal 108n
Patrides, C. A. 3, 13n, 59n
Paul 17, 18, 61, 78, 79, 83–4, 92
Payne, R. O. 36
Pearsall, D. A. 50, 59, 129
Pépin, J. 25n, 54
Personification 74–5, 119–20
Petrarch 57n
Petrus, id est, Christus 85–8
Philo 9–10, 16, 17, 19, 34n, 55
Piers Plowman 1–2, 4, 14, 28, 48, 49, 63–70, 71–131 *passim*
   and Anima 84–5, 88–92, 124–5

and Christ 85–8, 91–2, 93–5, 105–9, 110–11, 115, 119, 120, 122–8, 130
and Haukyn 123–5, 127–8
and History 73, 75–6, 79, 92–109, 122–6, 128–31
and Pardon 121–3
and Piers 77–9, 80–83, 85–109, 109–11, 113–31
and Poetry 63–70
and Tree of Charity 79–107, 125, 130
and Vision 63–70, 71–131 *passim*
Plato 52–3, 61, 78n
Platonism 7, 9–12, 15–19 *passim*, 39
Plotinus 3n, 18n, 78n
Ploughing imagery 109–25 *passim*, 128–31
Poets, Allegory of 4, 10–14, 19, 52–70 *passim*
Pontet, M. 16–17, 26n
Prestige, G. L. 26n

Quirk, R. 64n

Raban Maur 37, 87, 110
Ramsey, I. T. 13–14, 17n, 59, 100
Raw, B. 111n, 115n
Richard of Bury 116
Richard of St Victor 62
Richardson, A. 17n
Robertson, D. W. 2–6, 18, 27, 29, 35–6, 53–4, 55n, 71–2, 75, 82–3, 91n, 95, 97n, 103n, 109–11, 120, 126–8
Roques, R. 19n

Salter, E. 68n, 76, 89, 102, 105, 114n, 129

Salutati 57–8
Singleton, C. S. 11–12
Skinner, Q. 68n, 100n
Smalley, B. 17–18, 27–8
Smith, A. H. 77
Smith, B. 29n, 73–4, 83–4, 89, 101n
South English Legendary 112n

Theologians, Allegory of 4–5, 11, 15–32, 52–70 *passim*, 130
Thomas Aquinas 52–3, 56, 59, 61, 63, 93, 96–7
Three Middle English Sermons 33–8, 87
Time *see* History
Torrance, T. F. 109n
Travers, H. 126n
Trees 29–31, 47–9, 79–107, 130
Trinity 81–2, 97–9, 106
Trinkaus, C. 57–8
Troyer, H. W. 77
Tuve, R. 8, 42–6 *passim*, 49, 74, 75, 106n
Typology 7–8, 9–14, Chapter 2 *passim*
See also Allegory

Usk, Thomas 59, 89

Vasta, E. 77, 78–9
Vision 61–3, 64–70, 71–131 *passim*

Watson, E. 83n
Welter, J-T. 112n
Williams, N. P. 104n
Wind, E. 25n
Wittgenstein, L. 6